A Letter from a Gentleman to His Son Abroad
by Nathanael Torriano (The Elder.)

Address:
HardPress
8345 NW 66TH ST #2561
MIAMI FL 33166-2626
USA
Email: info@hardpress.net

A
LETTER
FROM A
GENTLEMAN
TO
His SON Abroad, &c.

ADVERTISEMENT.

AS there is a Confirmation in several Churches of this Kingdom, and as I hope this will not be thought an improper Book to be put into the Hand of the young Confirmed, so I thought this the most proper Time to send it into the World; and the more so, as I am credibly informed we have several already come, and more persecuted Refugees are daily coming, over here: And to such as these, surely, to shew the Pageantry and tinsy Gaudiness in which that WHORE of *Babylon*, the Church of *Rome*, is dressed, cannot but be grateful, whilst the Memory of her tyrannical Persecutions are still fresh upon them.

Not that I would here be understood in the least to favour the persecuting Spirit: No! far be that from the Breast of every Protestant, Layman or Divine, whose Breasts should rather be replete with the all-embracing Spirit of true CATHOLICISM, *taught* by that Redeemer who gave his Life a Ransom for ALL: And *enforced* by the Doctrines of that *Saviour*, who, whilst he concluded *all* under Sin, it was only that he might *have Mercy upon* ALL.

А. Н. Ку

IDDIO E IL MIO TORRIONE

Highmore Filius Pinx.   A. Walker Sculp.

Nathanael Torriano M.D.

A
LETTER
FROM A
GENTLEMAN
TO
His SON ABROAD.

OCCASIONED

By his having married a *Roman* Catholic.

To which are added,

A few MORAL and ENTERTAINING LETTERS, on different Subjects:

WITH

The PROTESTANT's Univerfal Prayer.

Ne impari jugo Copulamini. 2 Cor. vi. 14.

And they that are wife fhall fhine as the Brightnefs of the Firmament, and they that turn many to Righteoufnefs as the Stars for ever and ever. Dan. xii. 3.

The SECOND EDITION.

LONDON:
Printed for JOHN WREN, at the Bible and Crown, in Salifbury Court, Fleet-ftreet, 1757.

(Price 2*s*. 6*d*. Bound.)

T O

My Much-honoured and Affectionate MOTHER,

Mrs. *Elizabeth Torriano.*

Honoured MADAM,

AS I do not at all doubt but, on my First Birth-day, you dedicated me (by your fervent Prayers) to God, so I think it proper to acquaint you, that I have, at last, arrived to see one Birth-day, on the Employment of which I hope I may look back hereafter with Pleasure, whilst I reflect, that, in employing it to dedicate to you this Letter, I in Part return you the due Harvest from the Seeds of Education you have planted; though, perhaps, not so plentiful a Crop as might

be

be naturally expected from your careful Culture: *But every Ground will not yield an Hundred Fold.*

I truft, Madam, you will not only forgive, but be pleafed, and approve of, the Liberty I have taken, in dedicating to you a Book, which, I believe, you have long wifhed (*though never expected*) to fee in Print.

I am confident, Honoured Madam, you will, in its Publication, approve my Zeal for the Caufe of the True Religion: be pleafed with the due Refpect I pay my Father's Memory (*by no longer letting his Light lay under a Bufhel, but fetting it on a Candleftick*) and, at the fame Time, pardon my addreffing it to yourfelf: The Two firft need no Excufe; and, as to the laft, I have only to tell you, that, in a Dedication to yourfelf, I can never be accufed of any mercenary View, becaufe (the World knows, and I gratefully own, I have already been amply

paid

paid for this, and every other future Labour of my Life, by your Care of, and Tenderness towards, me; but most of all, for those Principles of religious Education, which (however I may, or may not, have improved them) I own I early received from you, and my late Honoured Father.

I assure you, Madam, I was very far from being at my *Ne plus ultra*, when I addressed it to yourself (as the Student was, who drank his Mother's Health because he knew no other Toast); for I am persuaded, my Father's innate Probity, his religious Principles, his known Veracity, the Desire of the * *East-India* Company to him, that

* The mentioning that Honourable Body, naturally reminds me gratefully to acknowledge how much we are obliged to them, for that kind Remembrance they still retain of the faithful, and by them approved, Services of my Father, by still continuing to employ, in their Service, one of his Sons, in the same Post he formerly filled; and, as it is his Third Voyage in their Service,

that he would once more accept of that laſt (and to his Family fatal) Embaſſy in their Service ; added to that general Applauſe he (*had then long ſince*) met with, when, on Account of the Peace of *Utrecht*, as well as in writing the *Britiſh* Merchants, he ſo ſtrenuouſly exerted himſelf in his Country's Cauſe, and made a Speech before the Houſe of Lords, which was, I think, honoured by Enrolment: All theſe, I ſay, Madam, make it abſolutely indiſputable that I could be at no Loſs where to find one, under whoſe Protection I might have ſent it into the World ; becauſe every one who knew him would have been pleaſed to have patroniſed any Work of his ; and I do not doubt (even from my unworthy Self) have gladly received a Dedication.

But, Madam, I thought it more your Due than any one living (and you

always

Service, confirms their Opinion of his Capacity and Integrity likewiſe ; which I humbly preſume he will never forfeit.

always taught me to be honeſt) not only as it comes from one, who owes you every Thing that Duty and Obligation can, but alſo as you know ſo perfectly the *(then to you melancholy)* Occaſion of its being wrote ; and have oft, no Doubt, ſhared in thoſe pungent Sorrows in my Father's Soul, that made him ſet about it ; and, at the ſame Time, have divided with him too thoſe Heart-eaſing Pleaſures which were the Conſequence *(in my Siſter's Converſion)* of its being wrote.

I have endeavoured to put it into ſuch a Form, as may make it moſt proper for the World's Peruſal, by leaving out all Anecdotes relative to Family only, which the World have no Buſineſs with ; and I ſhall greatly rejoice in (though not claim the Merit of) its Succeſs, ſhould it prove ſerviceable towards the rooting out Superſtition and Idolatry from amongſt thoſe who call themſelves Chriſtians, or preventing it in others ; or in the leaſt

a   give

give a Hint, in after Times, to such who may have Persons to educate, whose Education is of the *highest Confequence.*

If this my first publick Appearance should meet with your and the World's Approbation, you may expect, in a short Time, a larger Work in the *Polemical* Way; which I think I may very innocently throw into the Treafury of the Learned (as my Mite of Endeavour, and) as what I hope will be of such a Nature as will (should it ever appear) be free from the Cenfure, and meet with the Praife and Approbation, of the Worthy and Good, whofe Praife alone I am ambitious of.

Should any one afk, Why I added the Frontifpieces to fo fmall a Book? I anfwer, The Hiftory Piece was invented, and added, as an Inducement to fuch young Folks, into whofe Hands it might happen to come, to read the Book: The other was added (though other-

otherwife perhaps improperly) to let the World know, that whilft I am endeavouring to immortalize my Father's Memory, and publifhing any Thing which (though not relative to my Profeffion, yet) is againft the *worft*, and in Support of the *beft* Religion, I fhall never be afhamed to fhew myfelf in *Black* and *White* : — And happy fhall I think myfelf, if thefe my *Crotchets* (as they may be deemed) prove any way *Inftruments*, properly calculated, to extract thofe *falfe Conceptions* which I own I fear are too adhefive in the World.

In regard to the Letters I have added under fictitious Names, as there has been, fo there may be, Perfons fimilarly fituated ; and if fo, I hope a ferious Perufal of them may be of Service.—And I think I have a Right to fay what I do in the firft of them, fince I bear a kind of Relationfhip (tho' not by Affinity or Confanguinity) to one of his R—l H——fs's T——s,

a 2   who,

who, together with all his Family, received his firſt Principles of Erudition (as he has often been generous enough to own) from my Father. This is a known Truth; and therefore, I ſay, appears to me to give me a kind of Right to expreſs my Zeal in this (nationally) moſt intereſting Cauſe; and to raiſe in me the warmeſt Wiſhes that thoſe Seeds of Learning, which he cauſed to be ſown in ſo fruitful a Soil, may, as I do not doubt they will, when retranſplanted, be productive of every Thing which is great and good.

May it be long, Madam, ere you are permitted to ſee the by you much beloved Author in his bliſsful State; which (however ſelfiſh it may appear) is a Wiſh I cannot help making, becauſe in it is included, as a neceſſary Conſequence, your longer Life amongſt us; during which Time it is poſſible you may receive at leaſt the Signs of Gratitude, though not the adequate and reciprocal Marks of Affection and Duty,

Duty, from all your Children ; amongſt which (as none perhaps have been more obliged ſo) none is more deſirous of giving the moſt active Proofs of Gratitude, than is,

Honoured MADAM,

Your conſtant Companion, and

Moſt Obedient Son,

April 29, 1753.

N. TORRIANO, M. D.

P. S. This Letter ſhould have appeared in a more proper Attire : But that I think a Beauty needs no Velvet ; nor would a fine Dreſs excuſe its Publiſher's Deformities.

PREFACE.

AS the married State, when entered into in a religious and proper Manner, seems to bid the fairest of any other for our Comfort and Happiness, both here and hereafter; so is it equally likely to hazard both our present and future Welfare, when entered into without Consideration, for lucrative or lustful Views only, or merely to satisfy the sensual Appetites, and brutish Passions.

And, although there are many Things in Consequence of an Alliance so formed, which may (nay must) prove destructive to our Peace and Comfort here, and cast the Balance of Happiness against us, and make us risk the (as it were) dragging on Life with a disagreeable Companion, rather than living together like Two fond Hearts, united into one by the sacred Bonds of Wedlock, and those still stronger Ties of Affection; yet I think there is none in which we so much run the Hazards of our mutual Peace here and hereafter, as being

un-

unequally yoked together in our religious Principles.

This is a Misfortune of such a Nature, that it must *ever* the more increase, by how much the more the Parties really love : For the greater their Affections are, the greater in Consequence must their Afflictions be on each other's Account ; and the more Goodness, Piety, and Religion, is in either of them, the more Zeal they pursue their different Persuasions with, the more Misery, the more real Grief must either he or she feel at the one's being (as the other thinks) out of a State of Salvation.

This Difference must appear extremely plain upon a *professed Infidel's* marrying a *religious Christian* ; or, whenever a *professed Heathen* enters into that State with a bigotted *Mahometan* ; or, lastly, when a zealous *Turk* is joined, by the connubial Rite, to a stubborn *Jew :* Their Lives then must, surely, be like tying a dead Body to a live one ; or (like the Torments of *Mezentius*) on whom Death comes by slow Degrees :

Mortua quinetiam jungebat corpora vivis
Componens manibusque manus, atque ori-
bus ora.

But

But as thefe Differences are too glaring not
to be feen, and too ftriking not to be allowed, by every thinking Perfon : I will wave
thefe Diftinctions, and only fuppofe Two
Believers in the Chriftian Religion marrying together, who only differ in the Mode
and Form of their Worfhip : Two Chriftians, I fay, who have originally received
their Religion from the fame Head, and
Statutes from the fame Lawgiver, and who,
tho' they tell you they both follow the
fame Rock, and that *that* Rock is Chrift ;
yet are fo different in their Modes and
Formulas (by the Interpofition of human
Alterations, or Oral Traditions) that, I
am perfuàded, any utter Stranger could
hardly conceive any Thing *in Reality* fo
diametrically oppofite, where their appears
to be a nominal Samenefs.

And as, amongft thofe who call themfelves Chriftians, and who profefs to believe in the fame Redeemer, there are
many Sects who differ little, very little,
from each other, and that too only in
Non-effentials (in which Cafe a Union can
be no Hazard at all) I will fuppofe and
confine the Words of St. *Paul, Be not unequally yoked together*, to that Difference
only which fubfifts between a Proteftant
of the Church of *England*, who fhould
happen

happen to marry a Wife of the *Romiſh* Perſuaſion.

Let us ſuppoſe for a Moment, and reflect on the Confuſion which ſuch an Alliance muſt neceſſarily occaſion in their Family: How muſt it ſeparate them in their moſt ſerious Acts of Devotion, whilſt one is worſhipping *Paſte* or *Wood*, and the other adoring the *inviſible God?* What Hazards muſt their Children run of being erroneouſly educated, when the weaker Veſſel only, perhaps, has the Care of them, and ſhe too bigotted through Ignorance, and the Prejudice of that Education which her deluding Prieſts have abetted her in, and whoſe Zeal, though great, is not according to Knowledge, but, perhaps, a furious one (though well meant) which, in religious Matters, is always made the Support of a bad Cauſe, and too often of a good one (which would be much better ſupported by the calmeſt Reaſonings) as Truth is powerful, and will prevail.

I am the more induced to fix on the Inter-marriage of a Papiſt and Proteſtant, as my Thoughts have been pretty much heretofore engaged by the Subject of the following Letter, from my Father to my Brother (*whoſe Executors ſent it me after his Death*) who was exactly in this Situation.

He

He married a Lady, who was a Papiſt, and who went hence to the very Place where he was; which Marriage he having acquainted his Friends of here, occaſioned the following Letter to be wrote him by his Father; which I, having thus prefaced, ſhall ſend into the World (as all the Parties are dead) in Hopes hereby to ſupport the Cauſe of Religion and Virtue, to make Popery, diabolical Popery, appear in its proper Deformity; and the Proteſtant Religion, with all its native Purity, with all its rational Ornaments, and its every real Beauty.

I do not claim it as my own any otherwiſe, than that of my being its *Midwife*, to bring it into Light, and that of its *Nurſe* to dreſs (that is, moderniſe) it, ſince it came into my Hands, in a Manner fitter, as I humbly conceive, for publick View, than whilſt it was intermixed with many other Family Affairs, which the World has nothing to do with.

One Piece of ſecret Hiſtory however (*relative hereto*) which I myſelf knew, is, I think, neceſſary to be mentioned here by Way of Introduction, as a Hint, if not an Example, to others; which is, " That " the Two Perſons herein mentioned, at " Mar-

" Marriage made an Agreement, that they
" would never (after Marriage) talk of
" Religion, nor ever let it be the Sub-
" ject of Converfation, for fear the Heat
" of Bigotry fhould prove a ftronger Fire
" than the warmeft Affection.——This was
" ftrictly kept up to by both (as it was
" mutually agreed between them, that
" their Children fhould be fent over to
" *England*, and educated Proteftants).

" The Hufband, as was natural, was
" long uneafy and miferable at the fre-
" quent Vifits of Popifh Emiffaries, Priefts,
" *&c.* and yet kept to the Letter of his
" Word ftrictly, and only ufed now and
" then to drop Papers about the Houfe
" (in order that fhe might pick them up)
" containing Remonftrances of, and (to a
" rational thinking Mind) Confutations
" to, of many of the wicked Doctrines
" of the Church of *Rome*, and the moft
" material Matters of Difference between
" us and them.

" She (equally uneafy and diffatisfied,
" after having picked feveral of them up)
" broke the Ice firft, and begun firft to
" ftart religious Topics in Converfation :
" He readily met her half-yielding, half-
" inquiring Mind, and, for her Ufe, wrote
" a little Tract on Tranfubftantiation ;
" the

" the which she read, and seemed very
" much alarmed at; but yet desired to shew
" it her Priest, before she would intirely
" give her Assent to it: She did so (after
" her Husband had translated it into *La-*
" *tin*; which he did, for her Priest's Pe-
" rusal) whose only Answer was (and the
" only possible one indeed) *That if she*
" *wavered, all he could say to her would*
" *avail nothing.* This so staggered her,
" that she went no-where, as to a Place
" of Worship, for Three Years, but em-
" ployed herself at Home in reading all
" the Books of Controversy, *&c.* that she
" could get; and at last, by the Force of
" those Books, her Husband's kind Per-
" suasions, the Help of her own Reason
" and Reflection, and, above all, the
" Letter hereunto subjoined, she wrote
" Word over, That she had intirely for-
" saken the *Romish* Church, was intirely
" a Convert to Protestantism, and would
" on no Account, no nor the Gain of the
" whole World, again communicate there-
" with; and, as she was thus converted,
" the next Business she went about, was
" to follow the Advice our Lord gives
" to *Simon Peter, Luke* xxii. 31, 32.——
" where he tells him, *That Satan* (like the
" *Romish* Priest to her) *had desired to have*
" *him,*

" *him, that he might sift him as Wheat ;*
" *but he had prayed for him, that his Faith*
" *fail not ;* and then bids him, *when he*
" *was converted, strengthen his Brethren ;"*
and so it was with her : For she, too conscious how busy Satan had been, by his
proper and devoted Emissaries, the Popish
Priests, and how much they had endeavoured to sift her like Wheat, from every
good Principle, and leave her Soul only,
as it were, enchaffed, and but fit for
Fewel ; she, I say, in this Situation, wrote
to her own Family, with true religious
Rhetoric, beseeching them to be converted from the Errors of Popery, most fer-
vently desiring (as she most certainly did)
that their Souls might prosper, and be in
Health, even as she found experimentally
her's prospered : —— I say, experimentally ;
for surely (*morbus animi gravior est quam
corporis,* and consequently) if to get Rid
of any particular acute or chronic Disease,
or of a general Cachochymia in the Habit
of the Body, gives prodigious Ease to every Part, and, as it were, revivifies every
Function of Nature, How infinitely greater
must that mental Pleasure be, which re-
sults from having disburdened the Mind
of an intolerable Load of fallacious Inno-
vations in religious Matters, and a heavy
Yoke

Yoke of Superstitions ; which tend to nothing but to enslave the Mind, and prevent its every proper, every rational Exertion ; which all must certainly find to be the Case, who take upon them the easy Yoke of Christ's (pure, undefiled) Religion, instead of the slavish, arbitrary Bondage of Popish Bigotry.

Thus much by Way of Preface to the following Letter ; which, I hope, will be of universal Use to the Protestant Cause, by being a Guide to the unenlightened, and an Antidote ready at Hand for the Use of all, who are any Ways in Danger of being poisoned in their Principles, by the Contagion spread, but too universally, by the Popish Emissaries, amongst the Pagan World, and, I wish I was not obliged to say too, amongst those to whom that Light is sprung up, which was designed to be *the Glory of the* Israelites *of God.*

Farewel.

N. TORRIANO, M. D.

P. S. Should any one wonder why I acquaint the World, my Sister *was* a Papist ; let such an one be answered, by my telling him, *First,* I did it on purpose, pofe, that I might, at the fame Time, let them know fhe was converted upon Principle : *Secondly*, That, I believe, a Convert from Popery· may give as much Joy in Heaven as a converted Sinner, which is more than that arifing from Ninety-nine who need no Converfion : *Thirdly*, As a Perfon, who has a fine Jewel to expofe to View, which, tho' in its own Nature it is very bright, yet he chufes that every Diamond fhould have its proper Foil.——The Application is eafy.

A LET-

A
LETTER

FROM A

GENTLEMAN to HIS SON, Abroad.

DEAR CHILD,

SOME few Days after I had written you, by the *Stanhope*, a very short Letter, and promising this, giving you an Account that we had heard of your Marriage with ————, we received your Letter, of ————, by the *James and Mary*, which you writ us, to acquaint us therewith. I suppose those Letters will have reached you long before this; by which you will have seen the Surprize we were under, and the Concern it gave us, to hear you had married a Person of the Popish Religion, which I therein treated as a Religion little (if any Thing) better than Heathenism. And, though that Censure of it was writ on a Sudden, and upon the first Impressions of Concern, that were occasioned by the News of your Marriage, which we heard by the *Compton*, and before I

B   had

had received your Letter by the *James and Mary*, which was not then arrived : Yet I cannot, upon mature Reflection, think I have in the least wronged that Religion by the Comparison ; or, that we were too much surprised that you should marry one of that Religion.

I had so frequently recommended to you the changing your Condition, that you may be sure I was not in the least displeased at your being married ; nor yet that the young Gentlewoman you had married had no very large Fortune : For indeed, a Woman of any Merit (as I hear she is) is very rarely to be got, with any Fortune at all, in the *East Indies*. The Character she bears of a very modest and virtuous Person, suitable to the sober Education she has had, I should have thought Fortune enough there, had she had no other. And, as I am told she is of an agreeable Conversation, and possesses a great Share of good Sense, I should rather have applauded than discommended your Choice, even though she had not had a Penny, had it not been upon Account of her Religion ; which, I must own, is no little Disturbance to me.

I take it, that the Happiness of the married State does not consist so much in the Love of one another's Persons (though that is a very good Ingredient towards it) as in Affections much more lasting, those of reciprocal Friendship and Esteem : These strengthen and perfect the Happiness of the former, which will otherwise soon have an End. Uneasinesses and Discontents are the natural Parents of disesteem ; and, where Esteem is wanting, there can be no real or lasting Friendship.

ſhip. They muſt be Perſons of a very angelical Temper of Mind, in whom ſo great Differences in Religion do not cauſe Diſcontents and Uneaſineſſes: For the Tenderneſs that is, or ought to be, between Huſband and Wife, as it muſt occaſion the moſt ardent Deſires that the deareſt Part of themſelves, the Delight of their Lives, ſhould be happy, not only with them in this World, but more eſpecially in the next; ſo will it be the Foundation of an Uneaſineſs that muſt be as laſting at leaſt as their joint Lives, unleſs the one or the other of them change their Religion. For, the pungent Sorrow that muſt ariſe in each of their Souls, from the Belief that the other of them is in a wrong Way to eternal Bliſs, will ſour all the other Felicities of Life; becauſe, that next to the Concern and Sorrow that we ought to have for our own Sins, thoſe of our neareſt and deareſt Relations ought to affect us the moſt ſenſibly, and then, not the moſt flouriſhing outward Circumſtances in Nature can make us happy: And, where this Uneaſineſs, on ſuch a Reflection, is wanting, I believe true Love, whether it be conjugal, parental, or filial, muſt be wanting too. If, then, you and your Wife intend to be happy, you muſt, if you truly love one another, each of you endeavour to convert one another to that Faith which you reſpectively believe to be moſt agreeable to the Will of God, by all the Arguments that can be fairly drawn from Scripture and Reaſon; but without the leaſt Force, either directly or indirectly, made Uſe of: And, as ſuch an Endeavour muſt, till one has prevailed, be the Occaſion of many Con

teſts,

tefts, it will require the greateft Prudence fo to adapt the Strength of your feveral Arguments, as not to lofe one another's Affection by the Manner wherewith they are managed ; whereby you will be fenfible I had good Reafon to fay, in my former Letter, that, by thus marrying a Perfon of a different Religion, you had laid the Foundation of perpetual Contentions between you and the Perfon, whom, of all the World, you fhould be the furtheft from having any even the leaft Difference with.

Thus far I have enforced what I faid in my Letter by the ————, of the Uneafineffes that muft arife between Hufband and Wife, from their Differences in Religion ; but fhall wave faying any Thing more on the Subject of the Children you may have, feeing that, by the Letter I received from you by ————, you have given me your Word, that you will fend them over to be educated by me : So that, unlefs it happen that I die while they are young, the Religion of their Mother will not affect them, without it be by their own unfortunate Choice hereafter.

Another Thing I took Notice of to you, in the Letter already mentioned, was the Danger of fuch an Alliance to your own Faith. That fuch Marriages have been always thought ill of, we may learn from many Places in the Holy Scriptures. It is recorded of *Abraham* (a), that he made the Overfeer of his Houfe fwear by the God of Heaven and Earth, that *he would not*

(a) Gen. xxiv. 3.

take

take a Wife for his Son Isaac *of the Daughters of the* Canaanites ; and it is said (b) to be *grief of Mind,* not only to *Rebekah,* but also to *Isaac,* that their Son *Esau* had married with those Daughters of the *Canaanites* ; that is, such as worshipped not the God of *Abraham* and *Isaac.* And further, God by *Moses* (c) forbad the Children of *Israel's* intermarrying with those of an idolatrous Religion ; and, though it is possible there might be many other Reasons, both political and prudential, yet the only one there given by him, why they should not do it, is, the Danger of its leading them to Idolatry, as it is expressed in the next Verse, in these Words, *For they will turn away thy Sons from following me, that they may serve other Gods.* Now, though the Letter of the *Mosaical* Law be abolished, and that (for any Authority which that has over us) we are at Liberty to marry with whom we will, whether of one Religion or another, yet the Reason of that Prohibition will always subsist, which is, that we ought, out of a religious Fear, to abstain from those Sort of mixed Marriages, lest, by running ourselves into Temptations, we are over-persuaded either to forsake the Worship of the true God, or to worship him after a false Manner, or to give that Worship which is due to God, to that which is not God : Which is a Danger not to be thought light of, since the Scripture has given us a very eminent Instance of a Person, that had the greatest Reason imaginable to be the most fully persuaded of the Truth

(b) **Gen. xxvi. 35.**   (c) **Deut. vii. 3.**

of his Religion, who yet fell away, by the Pre-
valence of Temptation, in the very Cafe I am
now mentioning, That of marrying Wives of a
different Religion : For, though Almighty God
had twice appeared to (e) *Solomon* (which, one
would have thought, muft have worked in fo
irrefiftible a Manner upon his great Underftand-
ing, that no Temptation could have fhook him)
yet did his Wives draw him to Idolatry, and to
the forfaking of the true Religion, as appears
by his burning Incenfe, and facrificing to their
Gods (f). From whence we may learn, how
much it behoves us, though we are never fo
much perfuaded of the Truth of that Way of
Worfhip which we profefs, to take the greateft
Care poffible that we forfake it not; and to remember the Caution which St. *Paul* gives, the
Romans (g), *That, as we ftand by Faith, we fhould
not be high-minded, but fear* ; we fhould not be
too prefumptuous of our own Strength, or too
much poffeffed with an Affurance, that we cannot be overcome by fuch Temptations as have
overcome others : Which is a Caution I likewife
think reafonable to give you ; not becaufe I fuppofe you ready to fall from your Stedfaftnefs in
the Proteftant Religion (God knows my Heart
I both hope and believe otherwife) but with Defign to arm you with fuch a religious Fear, as
St. *Peter* fays (h) *is neceffary to enable us always to
be ready to give an Anfwer to every one that fhall
afk us a Reafon of the Hope that is in us* ; or that

(e) 2 Kings iii. 5.—ix. 2. (f) 2 Kings xi. 8.
(g) Rom. xi. 20. (h) 1 Pet. iii. 15.

fhall

shall enter into Controversy with us, concerning our Belief and Practice.

Perhaps it may, at first Sight, look somewhat too severe to say, as I did in my Letter *viâ Bombay*, That I did not forewarn you against marrying with one of the Romish Religion ; because I should have thought it as necessary to have forewarned you against marrying a *Jew*, or a *Mahometan*. But yet, upon Reflection, it will be found not too harsh : Since, if the religious Reason that God himself gave the Children of *Israel* against mixed Marriages, *viz. That they might not be a Snare unto them*, was good, the same will hold against all mixed Marriages that are equally dangerous, under the Christian, no less than under the *Mosaical*, Dispensation. But the Danger is the same, if the Sin to be avoided be the same, as I shall by and bye shew you it is. The prudential Reasons will likewise hold good as much in this Case as in the other, That the Unity of the Family may not be dissolved by the Heads of it taking different Ways in the Worship of God ; and that the Want of good Example may be no Encouragement to Prophanation or Contempt of Religion, in those committed to their Care ; besides the avoiding the continual Disagreements amongst themselves, that are likely to result therefrom. Nor can what St. *Paul* recommends to the *Corinthians*, who were, at that Time, married with Unbelievers (whether *Jews* or *Gentiles*) be a Justification for such mixed Marriages now, *viz.* (i) That the Husband was not to

(i) 1 Cor. vii. 10, 11, 12, 13.

B 4 put

put away his Wife, nor the Wife to leave her Husband, where the one of them happened to be called to Christianity, and the other not; because the Christian Religion, at its first Institution, found the World mostly in a married State; and therefore the dissolving such Marriages as were already solemnised, would have been to make the Gospel the Occasion of Confusion, instead of Peace: Besides, as he adds, it was not impossible, but the believing Person might be the Means of winning over the unbelieving; which, though a good Reason for continuing together when once married (as it might be a happy Result from an unhappy Circumstance) yet can hardly be thought such for coming together in these latter Ages.

I also charged the Popish Religion with having only the Name of Christian to distinguish it from Paganism. In Support of which Assertion, I will endeavour to fix Idolatry upon it, by shewing you, that the Church of *Rome* is really guilty of that Sin, notwithstanding it acknowledges the Trinity of Persons in the Unity of the Godhead.

The Sin of Idolatry may be committed either by giving, without the Permission of God, or contrary to his Commands, Divine Honour or Worship to any visible Image, or Representation of the Deity, believing the same to be God; which is the formal setting up an Idol in the Place of the true God; or, by believing that the Deity resides, or is present in, or with, such Image, Symbol, or Representation, and therefore using the same as an Object or Help to represent prefent him to our Minds ; which is worfhipping of him after a falfe and forbidden Manner : Or elfe, by putting our Truft and Confidence in any vifible or invifible Being, relying thereon, or praying thereto, as poffeffed of fome fupernatural Power for procuring us fome Good, or preferving us from fome Evil ; and therefore paying it that Honour which belongs to God, either fpiritually, by the inward Reverence of our Minds ; or materially, by fuch outward Actions of our Body ; at fuch Time as we are performing our religious Services, as are, by the common Ufe or Cuftoms of all Nations, underftood and taken to be the Acts of Worfhip proper to be given to God ; which is giving to a Creature the uncommunicated Honour of God.

Now, though the Romanifts may not be guilty of the firft Kind of Idolatry, the worfhipping the Image they fall down before, as believing it to be very God ; yet, if they are guilty of the latter, the worfhipping him after a falfe or forbidden Manner ; or the giving to a Creature, whether vifible or invifible, the Honour that is due to God, and uncommunicated by him ; they are certainly guilty of Idolatry.

The former is fo grofs a Notion, that we can hardly imagine even the Heathens themfelves to have been guilty of it : I fay hardly, becaufe I believe it is poffible there may be, or have been, fome of them brutifh enough to think a Stock or a Stone, or fome animated Creature, to be a God, as well as thofe *Jews*, whofe Stupidity the Prophet *Ifaiah* (k) reprefents as trufting in, or

(k) Ifaiah xliv. 17.

wor—

worſhipping their graven Images, and praying
to them to deliver them, as being their God.
Or as the *Egyptians*, who eſteemed the animated
Creatures Sheep and Oxen to be Gods, as may
be gathered from the Anſwer of *Moſes*, when
Pharaoh told him, they need not go out of the
Land of *Egypt*, but might ſacrifice to God where
they were ; to which he replies, That that muſt
not be, for they muſt ſacrifice ſuch Creatures to
God, as were eſteemed themſelves to be Gods
by the *Egyptians*, in whoſe Sight (1) ſuch Sacrifices would be ſo great a Scandal, and ſuch an
Abomination, as would provoke them to ſtone
them.

But the latter was the moſt generally practiſed,
both by Heathens and *Jews*, *viz.* the worſhipping the true God after a falſe or forbidden Manner ; or by giving divine Honours and Reverence
to any created, whether heavenly or earthly Being ; and praying to, and relying on, ſuch for
Safety and Protection.   That the Heathens did
ſo, is allowed by all Perſons that have inquired
into the Nature of their Worſhip ; many of
whoſe moſt celebrated Writers allowed of, and
pleaded for, the Inviſibility of God, though they
worſhipped him by an Image in the Form of a
Man, becauſe they thought Man the moſt ex-
quiſite Piece of Workmanſhip in this lower
World, and conſequently the moſt worthy to
repreſent the Deity to their Minds : And thoſe
of them that worſhipped the Sun, did it upon
the Notion that the Sun was that viſible Deity,

(1) Exod. viii. 25, 26.

by

by which the great God, who was invifible, ruled the World : Thofe likewife who worfhipped *Jupiter* as the Chief of their Gods, could not worfhip his Images, which they knew were very numerous, and fet up in almoft an innumerable Number of Places, out of a Perfuafion that each of thofe individual Images was that very God; but only as Reprefentations to which his Deity was adjoined, though they fuppofed his principal Refidence to be in Heaven, as may be gathered from moft of their poetical Writings. And the Emperor *Julian* the Apoftate, who was the Son of the firft Chriftian Emperor, *Conftantine* the Great, when after his Father's Death he apoftatized from Chriftianity to Heathenifm, fays in Excufe, or by way of Apology for his, and other Heathens worfhipping Images, That they worfhipped Images, not becaufe they thought them to be very Gods, but that by them, as Symbols or Reprefentations, they might worfhip the Gods.

The Idolatry of the *Jews* was alfo of this Sort ; of which I will give you fome Inftances. The Worfhip of the golden Calf may be brought as an Example of this Kind of Idolatry ; for *David* fays (m), *that they turned their Glory into the Similitude of a Calf that eateth Hay* ; that is, they worfhipped God, who was the peculiar Glory of the Children of *Ifrael*, by the Similitude of a Calf : For that this Image was only defigned by them as a Symbol or Reprefentation of God, may be gathered from the Story of it in *Exodus*, where the Children of *Ifrael* defired

(m) Pfalm cvi. 20.

to

to have a vifible Reprefentation of the Divine Prefence with them, faying to *Aaron* (n), *Make us Gods to go before us :* Had they defired it as the ultimate Object of their Adoration, and not rather as a Medium whereby to adore God, *Aaron* would doubtlefs never have confented to a Compliance with their Demand ; nor would they have propofed fuch a thing to him, who was the Prieft of God ; it was certainly a very heinous Sin in him to confent to make them any Reprefentation of God ; contrary to his exprefs Command delivered from Mount *Sinai* but a little before (o); but it would have been a much greater Sin in him to have made it as the final Object of their Worfhip ; as very God ! Befides, they had been brought out of the Land of *Egypt* by mighty Signs and Wonders, which they were fatisfied were wrought by the Power of an omnipotent Being ; and therefore could not poffibly believe the Calf, that they themfelves faw made and fafhioned before their Eyes, out of the golden Ear-rings which they gave *Aaron* for that Purpofe, could be that very God that had done all thofe Wonders for them. So that, when they cried out (p), *Thefe be thy Gods, O* Ifrael, *which brought thee up out of the Land of* Egypt (which is the very Preface that God was pleafed to make ufe of (q) before the Ten Commandments) they muft mean only, that they thought the Divine Prefence of that great and omnipotent God, which had brought them out

(n) Exod. xxxii. 1.   (o) Exod. xx. 4.
(p) Exod. xxxii. 4.   (q) Exod. xx. 2.

of

of the Land of *Egypt* with such mighty Signs and Wonders, and in so miraculous a Manner, was resident in or with that golden Calf. And this may be further gathered from what *Aaron* himself did at that Time ; for it is said, he built an Atar before it, and made Proclamation, saying (r), *To-morrow is a Feast to the Lord* ; where, by the Word *Lord*, is meant the Almighty God, because the Word there used is the Word *Jehovah*, which, I think, is generally allowed never to be used in the Holy Scripture, but when the Almighty God is spoken of.

The Idolatry of the Calves, which *Jeroboam* made and placed in *Bethel* and *Dan*, was also of this kind : For he made those Images, fearing the People might return to their old Master (s) *Rehoboam*, the King of *Judah*, if they should go up at the stated Times to sacrifice in the House of the Lord in *Jerusalem* ; to prevent which, it is said, he took Counsel, that is, he contrived to render their going up to worship at *Jerusalem* unnecessary, by providing them with visible Mediums, whereby to worship the invisible God, telling the People (t), that it was too much (too far) for them to go up to *Jerusalem*, but that nevertheless they might worship that God which brought them out of the Land of *Egypt*, by the Calves, the Symbols of his Presence, which he had caused to be made, and placed, for their greater Ease and Convenience, in those two Places. His offering Sacrifice before these Calves

(r) Exod. xxxii. 5.　　(s) 1 Kings xii. 27.
(t) 1 Kings xii. 28.

was

was paying divine Honour to a Creature, which is a Sin of fo heinous a Nature, as to be the Caufe that *Jeroboam* is feldom mentioned in Scripture without this particular Characterifstick, that it was he that made *Ifrael* to fin. For the Sin laid to his Charge was not the worfhipping thofe Calves as the final Object of his Worfhip, as being very Gods; but the worfhipping God by a Similitude, contrary to the fecond Commandment delivered to that People at Mount *Sinai*; for by that Commandment the outward and bodily Worfhip is forbid, as the inward and mental is by the firft. Nor could it be any Juftification of *Jeroboam*, that he intended the People fhould worfhip the true God by the Similitude of a Calf (as may be concluded from his ordaining Feafts (u) to be kept to them, like unto thofe which were in *Judah*) for whatever the Intention was, he was neverthelefs guilty of Idolatry, becaufe worfhipping any Similitude was forbidden (x); the tranfgreffing whereof was the Reafon of his being threatened to be fo feverely and exemplarily punifhed. It is alfo further to be obferved, that *Jeroboam* is blamed for having made Priefts of the high Places (y) out of the loweft of the People, which were not of the Sons of *Levi*; which he would not have been reproved for, had thofe Priefts been defigned to ferve before thofe Calves, as falfe Gods; but it was their being defigned to ferve before them,

(u) 1 Kings xii. 32. (x) Deut. iv. 15, 16, 17, 18. 1 Kings xiii. 4. xiv. 10, 11, 12, 13. (y) 1 Kings xii. 31. xiii. 33.

as

as Images of the true God, that made the appointing those Priests a Sin to *Jeroboam*. It was their being ordained to that Office, contrary to the positive Command of God (who forbad (z) that any besides the Children of *Aaron* and *Levi*, should minister in his Service) which occasioned the cutting off (a) and the destroying his Family from off the Face of the Earth. *Jehu* also served the Lord after the Manner of this forbidden Worship, and called the Priests of the Calves (b) *the Servants of the Lord*, in Contradistinction to the Priests of *Baal*, which last he utterly destroyed : The Worship of which false God was introduced by *Ahab*, with this emphatical Aggravation, that he was not content to continue the Worship of the Calves, which was the Sin of *Jeroboam* (c), but sinned yet more, for he brought in the Worship of the Image *Baal*, an Idol of the *Sidonians*, made in Honour of the Sun. And *Jehoram*, the Son of *Ahab*, though he followed the Sins of *Jeroboam*, is said (d), *not to have sinned like his Father* Ahab, *for he put away the Image of* Baal *which his Father had made*. And that the Priests of the Calves were those whom *Jehu* calls the Servants of the Lord, may be further gathered from hence, that he being King of *Israel*, and not of *Judah*, could have none of the Priests of the Lord of the Family of *Levi*, for he could not have any of the Children of *Aaron* for Priests, or of the other Branches of the

(z) Numb. i. 51. xviii. 22. (a) 1 Kings xiii. 34. (b) 2 Kings x. 23. (c) 1 Kings xvi. 30, 31, 32, 33. (d) 2 Kings iii. 2, 3.

House

Houſe of *Levi*, to miniſter in the other ſacred Offices; becauſe the Children of *Aaron* and the other *Levites* officiated only in the Temple at *Jeruſalem*, where the Worſhip of God was duly and rightly adminiſtered, according to his, own Appointment in the Law of *Moſes*.

The Inference that I ſhall draw from the long Account I have thus given of the Idolatry committed by the Children of *Iſrael*, in the Worſhip of the golden Calf in the Wilderneſs, and of thoſe that were made by *Jeroboam* upon the Separation of the two Kingdoms of *Iſrael* and *Judah*, is this, *viz.* That ſince God Almighty taxes the Children of *Iſrael* in both thoſe Inſtances with being guilty of the heinous Sin of Idolatry, though thoſe Images were made only as external Signs of God's Preſence amongſt them, and deſigned by them to be only Helps to their Devotion, by being viſible Repreſentations, placed before their Eyes, which that groſs People fancied they ſtood in Need of, to fix their Minds in the Adorations they were to pay to God Almighty by thoſe Mediums: The Papiſts are equally guilty of Idolatry, when they make uſe of any Images or Symbols placed before their Eyes, as intermediate Helps to fix their Thoughts upon God; who will have a truer and more ſpiritual (e) Worſhip paid to him; and who has not only forbidden all Attempts to liken or repreſent him under the *Jewiſh* Law; whether by Gods of Silver or Gods of Gold, or by

(e) John iv. 24. Iſaiah xl. 18. 25. Exod. xx. 23. Levit. xxvi. 1. Deut. v. 8, 9.

making

making of any Idol or graven Image, or Image of Stone to fall down thereto : But has alſo forbidden the ſame under the Goſpel Diſpenſation ; as we may ſee by the Preaching of St. *Paul* to the *Athenians,* when he tells them they muſt repent of thoſe Practices, ſeeing (f) *we ought not to think that the Godhead is like unto Gold or Silver, or Stone graven by Art or Man's Device.*

The Reaſon given by *Moſes* to the Children of *Iſrael,* againſt tranſgreſſing the ſecond Commandment, by attempting to make any Similitude of God, was, That when God was pleaſed to give them the Law from Mount *Sinai* (g), they *ſaw no Manner of Similitude* of any kind whatſoever. Now this Reaſon is as binding upon us Chriſtians ; ſince we are not only taught in ſeveral Places of the New Teſtament (h), to flee from Idolatry, and keep ourſelves from Idols ; but are likewiſe told, that God is inviſible, and that no Man hath ſeen God at any Time ; and that God is a Spirit, which it is therefore impoſſible adequately or properly to repreſent by any Thing that hath either Figure or Parts. It then the Papiſts, when they are at their Devotions, do make uſe of any Similitude whatſoever, though never ſo improper (for none indeed can be proper) whereby to repreſent God, or any of the Perſons in the Godhead, to their Minds, whether the Father, the Son, or the Holy Ghoſt, they are equally guilty of Idolatry, as well as the

(f) Acts xvii. 29, 30. (g) Deut. iv. 15, 16. (h) 1 Cor. x. 7, 14. 1 John v. 21. 1 Tim. i. 17. vi. 16. John i. 18. iv. 24. 1 John iv. 12.

C Children

Children of *Israel*. And that they do so in the Manner before-mentioned, they will not surely deny? or if they should, there are an innumerable Cloud of Witnesses to prove it upon them, that might be produced, not only out of ours, but even out of their own Authors: But I shall content myself to mention the Testimony of one Person only (which is to me in lieu of a thousand Witnesses) who told me he had several Times, in his Travels through *Italy*, seen the Picture of an old Man, a young Man, and a Dove, in the self-same Picture, set up in their Churches, Chapels, and religious Houses, made to represent the Trinity, which is the very Crime that St. *Paul* charges upon the Heathens (i), who changed the Glory of the incorruptible God into the Image of corruptible Man and Birds.

But though the *Romanists* should not make any Picture of the Father, or Holy Ghost, yet they are certainly guilty of Idolatry, whenever they bow down to, or pay any inward or outward Worship, or religious Reverence, to the Picture or Image of our Saviour, either upon the Cross, or otherwise visibly represented before their Eyes; whether it be expressed by kneeling or praying to, or before it, or by putting their Trust or Confidence in it, as believing his Divine Power or Presence adjoined thereto: As also when any Papists put any Trust or Confidence in their *Agnus Dei's*; which, after having been blessed by the Pope, are sent to Persons of

(i) Rom. i. 23.

that

that Communion to be kept as Safe-guards, to prevent Mifchiefs from befalling them, and to cure Difeafes; in Imitation of the Handkerchiefs or Aprons (k) that were carried from St. *Paul's* Body to the Difciples, who were thereby healed from their Difeafes, and preferved from the Power of evil Spirits: But this is now idolatrous, from the Expectation of a Bleffing and Protection to be derived to thofe, who fo place their Affiance, Truft and Confidence thereon; and is juft like the Practice of *Numa Pompilius*, the fecond King of *Rome*, who ufed to carry about with him, a Palladium, or Image of *Pallas*, as a Pledge to him of Empire; or of *Scylla* the Dictator, who in time of Battel always wore about him the Image of *Jupiter* or *Apollo*, as a fure Defence. The Figure of the Crofs, either with or without the Picture or Image of our Saviour upon it, reprefents him to us, as dead; for which Reafon (were there no other) it is a very improper Medium to pray, or pay our Adorations to him by: Our Prayers are to be made to him, as he is glorioufly reigning in Heaven, which cannot poffibly come under any Reprefentation whatever; becaufe we can have no Notion how tranfcendently glorious he is there; and therefore all Attempts to reprefent him in that State would be vain; and, fince we firmly believe him to be God bleffed for ever, would be alfo idolatrous; as being within the Prohibition of not worfhipping God by any Similitude whatfoever.

(k) Acts xix. 12.

I am

I am not infensible of the Apology made by fome of the modeftteft of the *Romanifts*, for this Practice, *viz.* That they do not fall down to, or before, the Image of our Saviour on the Crofs; or to that other Reprefentation of him, when pictured in the Likenefs of a young Man with a Glory round him, either fitting in Heaven, or afcending thither; with Defign to give Honour to the inanimate Picture or Image of Gold, Silver, *&c.* but only with Defign by the firft to bring to our Rembrance the Agonies which our Lord endured for our Sakes; and by the other, the Advantages he has procured for us by his Refurrection. Were there abfolutely no further Ufe made of them, I fay *abfolutely* no other, or bad, Ufe made of them, I cannot fay they would be Idols; becaufe the bare making fuch a Picture, Image, or Statue, free from all Manner of Intention to bow down, or pay any religious Reverence or Worfhip to it, is not making an Idol; any more than the making the Picture, or Statue of fome great Warrior, Philofopher, Legiflator, or other extraordinary Perfon, as of *Alexander*, *Ariftotle*, *Lycurgus*, or others (in Memory of their great Victories; the ufeful Philofophy, or the admirable Laws they taught Mankind) can be called making an Idol, when no Proftration, or other religious Ceremonies are made to them. And therefore the Pictures of our Saviour and his Apoftles in the Chartons of *Raphael*, which hang up in the Gallery at *Hampton-Court*, not as Pictures to be worfhipped, but as hiftorical Pieces, or Monuments of the Miracles there reprefented; I fay, thofe Pictures being

placed

placed there with this latter Defign *only*, may very innocently be kept there. Nor can the Pictures of *Mofes* and *Aaron* in the Proteftant Churches ; or of our Saviour and his Apoftles in our Common Prayer-books, be called Idols, be- caufe we never pay them any inward Worfhip of the Heart, or outward Reverence of the Body. However, I muft freely own, that in my private Opinion they had all of them much better be laid afide, becaufe of the Offence and Scandal thereby given to our Diffenting Brethren, who are grieved at this Cuftom ; and we are to give no Offence, neither to the *Jew*, nor to the *Gen- tile, nor yet* (furely) to the Church of God, which the Diffenters are as much as ourfelves, though the *Romanifts* are not ; the continuing whereof, when we may fo fafely, and without Detriment, remove the former out of our Churches, and leave the latter out of our Books, is, I think, contrary to the Advice of St. *Paul* in his Epiftles to the *Romans* and *Corinthians*, where he pleads for our having great Regard (1) to our weak Brethren ; and at leaft perfuades us very ftrongly, if he does not command us, to wave what may perhaps be ftrictly lawful for us to do, for that which may be more expedient, or more edifying to others, and particularly in- ftances in Meats offered to Idols. His Argument runs thus, That although a Man who knows that an Idol is nothing, may, *without wounding his own Confcience*, eat of the Meats offered to it ; yet he is to abridge himfelf of that Liberty, if fo be that his ufing it is an Offence to his

(1) Rom. xv. 1, 2.   1 Cor. x. 23, 24.

C 3

weak

weak (or fcrupulous) Brother. The Cafe, I think, is the fame with relation to the Pictures that are in our Churches and Common Prayer-books before-mentioned, which may not indeed be unlawful for us to have there, becaufe we make no ill Ufe of them, as we pay no religious Service to them; but are not expedient or edifying, in as much as they give Offence to other good, though fcrupulous People; and therefore, I think, ought to be removed from our Books of Devotion, and Places fet apart for religious Worfhip, feeing our Brethren are fcandalized thereat. But this is not the Cafe of the Church of *Rome*, for there, a further Ufe is made of them, and that a very criminal one too! For *by that Church* they are thought to be poffeffed of fome inherent Holinefs; and to be facred Repofitories of fome divine Powers, or Virtues adhering to them, in the Efteem not only of the moft ignorant or lefs knowing Papifts (whofe Souls ought not to be expofed to fuch imminent Danger) but even in the Opinion of fome of their moft learned Men, who are guilty of paying divine Worfhip to the very Pictures and Images of the Crofs or Crucifix, or to thofe of the Apoftles, and other fuppofed Martyrs and Saints.

It is notorioufly known, that there are at this Day in Popifh Countries, and that there were in our own Country before the Reformation, many Pictures and Images of our Saviour, of his Crofs, of the Virgin *Mary*, of the Apoftles, and of other Saints and Martyrs fet up in Churches and Places of religious Worfhip, with Defign that the People fhould fay their Prayers to, or at

least

leaft before them ; nay even in the * Highways and Streets of the greateft Concourfe are thofe Images fet up with the before-mentioned De-fign : Which, I think, bares a very great Re-femblance to the high Places (m) and Groves, &c. appropriated by the idolatrous *Jews* to the Worfhip of their Images : For to, or (as the *Romanifts* chufe to diftinguifh) before the Pic-tures or Images fo placed, do the *Romanifts* make fuch Geftures of the Body as are the proper Signs of Adoration and Worfhip.

If I fhould then afk the Papifts, Whether the Geftures of kiffing the Images or Pictures ; or of bowing or kneeling to them ; or of praying to or before them ; are Acts of Devotion done with regard to thofe Pictures or Images alone ? Or to God alone ? Or to God and the Images, &c. conjointly ? They would not, I fuppofe, an-fwer, that they are done in regard to the Image alone, fince that would be confeffing themfelves guilty of the *groffeft* Idolatry : For fince it can-not be pretended in Excufe thereof, with the leaft Colour of Reafon, that thofe Actions are done to, or before the Image, &c. of fuch or fuch Perfons out of any civil Refpect, becaufe the Perfons reprefented by thofe Images, &c. are dead, or becaufe the Perfons that are paying thofe Signs of Refpect, are then at their Prayers, and paying their religious Service to fome Being ; it

* In *Moorfields* not two Years ago, I believe in 1750, there then remained a Crofs : At which I make no doubt there formerly was Devotions paid by the illiterate Fools of the Church of *Rome*.

(m) 1 Kings xi. 7. 2 Kings xxi. 3, 4.

C 4

muft

muſt therefore follow, that they are performed as Acts of Devotion ; and conſequently do render the Performers *truly* guilty of Idolatry. For the inward Perſuaſion of the Mind being only to be known and diſcovered to us by the outward Actions of the Body ; and the outward Actions of the Body cauſing the Beholders to believe, that the inward Senſe of the Soul is congruous to ſuch outward Actions ; is the Reaſon why God, who is jealous of his Honour, will not ſuffer the outward Geſtures of the Body to be paid to any Image, *&c.* whatſoever ; and has ſo often in Scripture forbidden the bowing down (n) or falling down to any Image, *&c.* ſince that would, not only in his own Sight, but in the Sight of the Beholders, be giving his Honour to a Creature.

Nor will they, I preſume, ſay, that thoſe Actions are done with regard to God alone, becauſe they have at that Inſtant their Eyes lifted up to, and fixed upon, the viſible Object before them, as the *Jews* had upon the golden Calf, made with Deſign to go, or be, before them, *i. e.* to be viſibly preſent in their Sight. Beſides, ſuch an Anſwer cannot, with any Colour of Truth, be made by any knowing Papiſt that has acquainted himſelf with the Canons and Orders of that Church ; for the Miſſal of that Church commands the Prieſt in expreſs Words *(o),* after he has fixed the Croſs in the Place prepared for it before the Altar, *to pull off his Shoes, to bow to it, and then kiſs it :* And in the Pontifical, at

(n) Exod. xx. 4.   Lev. xxvi. 1.   Deut. v. 9.
(o) Rom. Miſſal, p. 182.

the

the Benediction of a new Crofs, the Bifhop is required in exprefs Words (p), *to-bow his Knee before it, and devoutly to adore it !* All which-Ceremonies are Signs of Adoration and Worfhip, when performed on a religious Account ; though, when they are performed on other Accounts, as to our Prince, or on any other civil Occafion, they are Marks of our civil Refpect only ; but even in this Cafe were better let alone, in my humble Opinion.

The Ceremony of pulling off the Shoes is a Piece of religious Reverence and Honour, which God appropriated to himfelf, by commanding *Mofes* to put off his Shoes when he fpoke to him out of the Midft of the burning Bufh ; for though it might be an Angel, *properly fo called,* that put on the Appearance of (q) a flaming Fire, to draw *Mofes's* Attention, yet it was God that (r) fpoke to him, as may be feen from the following Verfes of that Chapter, when he tells him, that it was God, whofe Name was *I am,* that fpoke to him, and fent him to *Pharaoh* and to the Children of *Ifrael* in *Egypt,* which Name is applied by our Saviour to himfelf, in his Difpute with the *Jews* in the eighth Chapter of St. *John* (s) ; and is likewife afcribed to him in the fame Signification, though in other Words, by the Apoftle to the *Hebrews* (t), when he fays of Jefus Chrift, that he is *the fame Yefterday and To-day and for ever,* i. e. always, I am. And, that it was not an Angel (at leaft not an Angel pro-

(p) Rom. Pontif. p. 164, 165.
(q) Exod. iii. 2.   (r) Exod. iii. 4. and 14.
(s) John viii. 58.   (t) Heb. xiii. 8.

perly fo called, *viz.* a created Spirit) but the *Word* of God, the *only begotten Son of God, our Saviour,* who is in Scripture fometimes called Meſſenger (u) or Angel ; as alſo the Preſence of God ; and the Angel of his Preſence ; and whom the Apoſtle to the *Hebrews* ſtiles *the Brightneſs of God's Glory ; and the expreſs Image of his Perſon* ; and who muſt have been meant, when it is faid, that *Moſes* (x) fhould behold the Simi-litude of the Lord, who would ſpeak to him. Mouth to Mouth ; and whom he had ſeen Face to Face. I fay, we may certainly conclude it was not a created Angel, that ſpake to him, from St. *Stephen*'s making this very Diſtinction, at his Defence before the High Prieſt and Council of the *Jews*, that it was (y) an Angel of the Lord that appeared to *Moſes* in a Flame of Fire in the Bufh, but it was the Lord that bid him put off his Shoes from off his Feet : And a little lower, fays of our Saviour (whom he there calls that Prophet that was to be raiſed up like unto *Mo-ſes*, and whom they were to hear) that he was (z) the Angel that ſpake to *Moſes* in Mount *Si-nai.* From which Paſſages I infer, that this Honour of pulling off the Shoes, is no where in Scripture communicated to any created Being ; and conſequently, that the paying that Honour to a Croſs, or to any other Creature, is giving it the Honour appropriated to God alone : For the Perſon who is erroneouſly, in the *Contents* of the fifth Chapter of *Joſhua*, ſtiled an Angel, is

(u) Mal. iii. 1.   Exod. xxxiii. 14.   Iſaiah lxiii. 9. Heb. i. 3.   (x) Numb. xii. 8.   Exod. xxxiii. 11. (y) Acts vii. 30. and 33.   (z) Acts vii. 38.

called

called in the *Text* of that Chapter (where he appeared to *Joshua* at the Siege of *Jericho*, and bid him put off his Shoes from off his Feet) the (a) Captain of the Hosts of the Lord; and both in the *Contents* and *Text* of the *next* Chapter, the Lord; by whom must be intended, the (b) Word of God, whom the Armies in Heaven followed. And that he was so, the Word of God, whom St. *John* tells us (c) was God, we may further conclude from hence, that when *Joshua* fell on his Face to worship him, he did not forbid him to do it, as the Angels (properly so called) and the Apostles of our Lord always did, whenever any outward Signs of religious Worship were offered to be paid to any of them; as we may see by what was said by the Angel to St. *John* in the *Revelations* (d); and by St. *Peter* to *Cornelius*; and by St. *Paul* and St. *Barnabas* to the People at *Lystra*.

And as to the kneeling to, or before, the Images of the Cross, *&c.* they are exactly the same religious Ceremonies that were used by the idolatrous *Jews* to their Images; as is intimated in that Passage, where God tells the Prophet *Elijah*, That he had (e) left in *Israel* seven thousand, which were all the Knees that had not bowed to *Baal*, and every Mouth that had not kissed him. From whence it appears, that in the Opinion of God these outward Actions performed to a Creature were the characteristical

(a) Joshua v. 14, 15. vi. 2. (b) Rev. xix. 13, 14, 16. (c) John i. 1. (d) Rev. xix. 10. xxii. 9. Acts x. 26. xiv. 14, 15. (e) 1 Kings xix. 18.

Marks

Marks of an idolatrous Worſhip ; and the **Rea-**
ſon why thoſe who performed them were eſteemed Idolaters, which was ſo provoking a Sin *in*
the Sight of God.   Since then the performing
ſuch outward religious Ceremonies, before their
Images, were ſufficient to denominate the *Jews*
Idolaters in the Judgment of God, there can be
no good Reaſon aſſigned, why the *Romaniſts,*
who perform the ſame religious Ceremonies before their Images, ſhould not be eſteemed Idolaters too.   For it muſt always be remembered,
That the outward idolatrous Ceremonies of the
Body, are as much forbid by the Second, as the
inward idolatrous Thoughts of the Heart are by
the Firſt Commandment :   And, that he who
trangreſſes any one of the Commandments of
God *(f)*, is equally guilty of tranſgreſſing a
Commandment, with him who tranſgreſſes any
other of them.

Neither, ſurely, will they . ſay, That it is
done, with regard to God and the Image, *&c.*
conjointly : Becauſe, whatever Degree of that
divine Worſhip is paid to the Crucifix or Image,
&c. of Chriſt, is paid to a Creature ; unleſs they
will ſuppoſe, that the Divinity of our Saviour is
ſo perfectly united to the Image, *&c.* as to change
or remove the very Subſtance of Gold or Silver,
&c. and to tranſubſtantiate it into the Godhead :
A Thing that, I think, the greateſt Sticklers
for this Practice have not the Front to affirm !
And yet, unleſs that can be proved, it will follow, that ſome religious Worſhip or Service is
paid to the Creature then preſent before them,

(f) James ii. 11.

con-

contrary to the Second Commandment, which prohibits the bowing down to any made Likenefs of the Godhead (g); as well as to our Saviour's Explanation of the Firft Commandment, that God, and God only, was to be worfhipped (h). If then God only be to be worfhipped, that Worfhip muft needs be idolatrous that has any Thing for its Object, either feparately from, or conjointly with, God, but God alone.

The common Excufe that is made for this Practice is, that the outward Actions of bowing, &c. to the Crofs, or Image of Chrift, is not made to it with Intention to give the fame Degree of Honour to the material Image, &c. as to the Perfon of Chrift reprefented thereby ; and that therefore, there being only an inferior Degree of Honour paid thereto, it cannot be Idolatry. To which I anfwer, That this is no Excufe, becaufe it is contrary both to the Meaning and Letter of the Command, that any, the leaft as well as the higheft, Degrees of Honour fhould be paid to a created Similitude of God ; and might as well have been formerly pleaded by the *Jewifh* and *Heathen,* as now by the *Chriftian* Idolaters : For the glorious Majefty of God is as well affronted by the leaft, as by the higheft, Honour given to any Image, &c. of him ; becaufe, to all Appearance, Adoration is paid to the Similtude, whenever thofe lower Degrees of Honour are paid to it, as really as if the higher Degrees of the Worfhip of the Heart were joined thereto ; the By-ftander, who is not able to

(g) Exod. xx. 4, 5.   (h) Matth. iv. 10.

dif-

difcern the Secrets of the Heart, always fuppofing them to go together. Befides, whatever People may fanfy, this is fo very nice and fubtle a Diftinction, as feems impoffible to be truly made, or the Degrees of Worfhip to be fo really divided (if that would do the Bufinefs) as not to confound the Imagination of the very Perfon performing it; efpecially if he be of the common Mafs of Mankind, and not extremely well verfed in diftinguifhing of Ideas; and utterly impoffible for a *Jew*, a *Turk*, or a *Pagan*, who fhould be prefent when the *Romanifts* are performing their Devotions before the Crofs, or Crucifix, or before any Image or Picture of our Saviour, or of the Virgin *Mary*, or any of the Apoftles, or other He or She Saint, to judge otherwife than that fuch *Romanift*, as well as the *Jewifh* or *Heathen* Idolaters of old, really adored thofe Figures or Reprefentations, to or before whom they performed their Devotions; if not as real Gods, yet at leaft as vifible Reprefentations of the Deity; or as believing his Prefence, or fome holy and fupernatural Power or Virtue refident therein. This Part of their Religion muft be certainly contrary to what Chrift came into the World to teach us; for the End of his coming into the World was to teach us to abolifh, not to continue, Idolatry; to teach us to forfake thofe Vanities (the worfhipping of Idols) and to turn to the living God; as we may learn from St. *Paul*'s Difcourfe to the *Athenians*, where he tells them, that it was the Intent of God in ordaining his Son to be the Judge of the World, that all Men fhould repent, and not think that

God

God was like Gold or Silver, &c. (i) but that they fhould ceafe to worfhip him after that ignorant Manner which they had practifed in Times paft. But, fuppofing only Chriftians were to be Spectators of their Worfhip, how few of us are capable of judging other than by Appearance? And why muft the great Doctors (if they themfelves are capable of making thefe Diftinctions) be permitted to lay fuch Stumbling-blocks in the Way of the common People, who have, for the moft Part, dull and heavy Underftandings, and who, by their grofs Ignorance and Inadvertency, are very fufceptible of wrong Impreffions, and will be apt to think there is a relative Honour due to the Images, &c. themfelves : For, as we find by Experience, that bad Examples are of more Force than good Precepts ; fo, the feeing thefe outward Genuflexions, and other Marks of Adoration, paid by their Priefts and learned Men to thefe falfe Objects of Worfhip, will be more prevalent to induce them to follow the dangerous Examples of fuch bold Guides, than the moft pious and cautious Exhortations will be to deter them from following fuch prefumptuous and idolatrous Practices. It is very much to be feared, that moft of the ignorant People in that Church believe there is at leaft a Tranfition of Worfhip, by or through the vifible Medium to the invifible God, being ignorant of the fubtle Diftinctions which the Men of Learning pretend to make therein ; though that cannot poffibly be any Excufe even for them, againft the pofitive

(i) Acts xvii. 29, 30.

and

and plain Prohibitions contained in fo many Places of Scripture, of ufing no Manner of Similitude in the Worfhip of God, who is a Spirit, and will therefore be worfhipped after a fpiritual Manner. How uncharitable then the Continuance of this Practice of worfhipping Chrift by a bodily Refemblance is, that Church (which commands the Performance of it) ought to think of with the greateft Humiliation and Repentance, feeing the great Likelihood there is, that Multitudes of Souls will be eternally loft by following fuch dangerous and idolatrous Practices.

But, from being Spectators of the outward Actions practifed in the Worfhip of Images, &c. in that Church, let us pafs to the Words that compofe the Prayers, that are not only put up before thofe Images, &c. but are directly addreffed to them (i); which are as full, ftrong, and expreffive, of the inward Adoration of the Heart, as it is poffible to ufe in the moft proper Adoration of God the Father, or of Jefus Chrift our Lord : Such as thefe which follow to the Virgin *Mary*; which are to be found in the Book of Offices, or Service to her, fet forth by Pope *Pius* the Vth, where fhe is worfhipped in the following Words : (k) *Eftablifh us in Peace. Unloofe the Bonds of the Guilty. Drive away our Evils. Make us abfolved of our Faults, meek and chafte. Vouchfafe us a fpotlefs Life. O facred Virgin, give me Power againft thy Enemies. Let the Virgin*

(i) See more of this in the Poftfcript.　(k) Offices for the Virgin, Pfal. lxxxix. xcvi. cii. ciii. cvii.

Mary

Mary, *blefs us, and our pious Offspring.* Mary, *Mother of Grace, Mother of Mercy, do thou defend us from the Enemy, and receive us at the Hour of Death.* Thefe Prayers, in the plain and moft obvious Signification of the Words of them, are a direct Calling upon the Perfon addreffed to in a pofitive, not in an interceffory Manner, to blefs, to help, to affift, to forgive, and to confer Grace upon, the Supplicant, nay and even to fave him in the Hour of Death. In what Words muft I addrefs myfelf to God, if thefe are to be put up to a Creature? If thefe are not Forms of Prayer, expreffing an abfolute Truft, Confidence, and Reliance, in the Perfon prayed to, I muft own myfelf ignorant enough not to underftand what Words to make Ufe of for fuch a Purpofe! There are Abundance of other Paffages in that Book which fpeak the fame Language; and in other Popifh Books there are fuch an incredible Number of Prayers, not only to the Apoftles, but to other real or pretended Saints, as render it impoffible to tranfcribe, had I the Books by me to do it from: But I thought fit to give this Sample of their Invocations and Prayers to the Virgin *Mary*, whereby it may appear, that the fame Veneration, Affiance, and Devotions, are placed in, and paid to her, as are due only to God; and which cannot poffibly admit of any other Conftruction, than that they are a plain and direct Form of Worfhip and Adoration paid to a Creature; which whofoever is guilty of doing, cannot avoid the Guilt of Idolatry.

D   Another

Another Way by which we may be guilty of the Sin of Idolatry, befides that of the Worfhip of vifible Images, &c. is the putting our Truft and Confidence in any invifible Beings befides God himfelf, and praying to them as poffeffed of fupernatural Power for procuring us fome Good, or preferving us from fome Evil; either properly in their own Power to confer, or thought to be procurable by their Mediation; by which that Honour is afcribed to them which is properly belonging only to God and Chrift. The Papifts are guilty of this Sort of Idolatry when they pray to Angels, or the Virgin *Mary*, or other Saints, to be Mediators between God and them, or between Chrift and them; or, as their Benefactors to confer upon, or procure for them, fome Good, or to deliver them from fome Evil. For, though they may not, perhaps, fometimes pray to them with the very fame Affiance as they do to God and Chrift; or may not afcribe to them the higheft Honour which they believe due to God and Chrift; yet, if they put their Confidence in them, as that, by their Power or Mediation, they fhall obtain fuch Things as they pray to them for; they thereby afcribe to them fuch religious Honour as is difproportioned to them; and above what can be due to any created Being; and what God has not communicated to them, or commanded to be paid them (l), but has referved to himfelf. For Example: We are told in Scripture (m), that the *only Mediator be-*

(l) Deut. xvii. 3.　　　(m) 1 Tim. ii. 5. Col. i. 20.

tween

*tween God and Man, is the Man Chrift Jefus;
by whom it pleafed the Father to reconcile all Things
to himfelf.* Whenever, therefore, without an
exprefs Warrant from God, delivered in Holy
Scriptures, which is the only Rule to go by, the
Papifts fhall pray to any Angel or Saint to be
their Mediators, they thereby afcribe to them
the Honour of Mediation, which is appropriated
to Chrift alone, who is God *bleffed for ever* (n).
Again, whenever they pray to any Angels or
Saints departed, as their Proteƈtors, Patrons or
Patroneſſes, they do it without Warrant from
God, and afcribe to them that Proteƈtion which
proceeds from God only (o). And God, who
is jealous of his Honour, as he has told us in the
xxth Chapter of *Exodus* and the 5th Verfe (p),
will not permit us to give his Glory to a Creature, but has commanded us, by the Apoftle
St. *Paul* (q), to take care that we do not fuffer
ourfelves to be *beguiled of our Reward by a vo-
luntary Humility, and worſhipping of Angels*;
notwithftanding they are the higheft and moft
excellent of all his Creatures. And although,
in many Places of Scripture (r), mention is made
of the good Offices that are frequently done for
Men by the Miniftry of Angels, and of their
tarrying round about them that fear the Lord;
and delivering them from Harm; yet we no
where read, that any of thofe good Men, that
were eminently preferved by their Miniftry, ever

(n) Rom. ix. 5.　　(o) Deut. xxviii. the whole
Chapter.　Pfal. cxxi. the whole Pfalm.　　(p) Exod.
xx. 5.　　(q) Col. ii. 18.　　(r) Gen. xxxii. 1, 2.
Pfal. xxxiv. 7.　Aƈts xxvii. 23.

returned the Angels any Thanks or Praife for their having protected them from Mifchiefs; but their Prayers and Praifes were returned to God, who was the Author of that Good which the Angels were only the Minifters or Inftruments of; as we may fee by the Example of the Prophet *Daniel* (r), who, when the Lions were with-held by the Angel of God from doing him any Harm, afcribes his Prefervation to *God*, who had *fent* his *Angel* to fhut the Lions Mouths; but pays no Thanks to the Angel, who was no otherwife concerned therein, but as a *Meffenger* or *Minifter* of God, fent for that Purpofe. The Vifion of the Horfes and Chariots of Fire, which was feen by the Servant of *Elifha* (s), was an Appearance of the Angels of God in the Likenefs of an Hoft or Army; from which nothing more can be concluded, but that the Hoft of God is more numerous and powerful than the greateft Armies of Men; and that God is pleafed to fend his Angels to protect his Servants from the moft imminent Dangers; or to punifh his Enemies in the moft exemplary Manner; the Praife and Honour whereof is only due to him, by whofe good Pleafure they are fent to protect and defend the Righteous, or to punifh and deftroy the Wicked. And in the New Teftament we are taught, by the Apoftle to the *Hebrews* (t), that Angels are *miniftering Spirits*, fent forth to minifter to them who fhall be Heirs of Salvation; as were thofe Angels that appeared either

(r) Dan: vi. 22.   (s) 2 Kings vi. 17.
(t) Heb. i. 14.

to

to *Cornelius* (u), informing him what he was to do; or to St. *Peter* (x), delivering him out of the Hands of *Herod*, and from all the Expectation of the *Jews*; or to St. *Paul* (y), encourageing him in his Voyage, and assuring him, that God would preserve all those that sailed with him; as likewise those, whom we may suppose to be more peculiarly appointed to watch over young Children in their Infancy (z), to preserve them from the many Dangers which, by Reason of their Youth, Inadvertency, and Want of Experience, they would otherwise be liable to fall into. From whence we acknowledge them to be ministring Spirits, according to the Will of God; and that, therefore, no Worship or Thanks is to be paid to them, but to God only, for the good Offices which they do us. And accordingly our Church, in the Collect for *Michaelmas-day*, prays to God (a), *That, as his holy Angels always do him Service in Heaven, so, by his Appointment (not by their own Will) they may succour and defend us here on Earth.* Since therefore it is by God's Appointment that they are serviceable to us, they are not to be worshipped as our Protectors or Benefactors, not so much as by the external Actions of the Body, much less by the internal Devotions of the Soul; but God only ought to be the Object of our Worship. This we may learn from that Passage of the *Revelations* (b) already mentioned, where the Angel

***

(u) Acts x. 4, 5.   (x) Acts xii. 7. 9.   (y) Acts xxvii. 23, 24.   (z) Matt. xviii. 10.   (a) Collects for *Michaelmas-day*.   (b) Rev. xix. 10.

        severely

feverely rebukes St. *John* for offering at fuch a Thing : And the Reafon he there gives will hold good, not only againft all Angel-worfhip, but againft the Worfhip of any real or fanfied Saint, or created Being, whatfoever, *viz. See thou do it not, for I am thy Fellow-fervant.* And, in the laft Chapter of that Book, when St. *John* was relapfed again into his former Error, and fell down to worfhip before the Feet of the Angel, he again tells him (c), *See thou do it not*, for the fame Reafon as before, *that he was his Fellow-fervant, and of his Brethren the Prophets, and of them which kept the Sayings of that Book* ; and further adds, *That he fhould worfhip God*, that is, God only. As if he had faid, You are in the Wrong to offer to worfhip me, by falling down before me, how glorious foever I may feem in your Eyes, for I am really no more than one of God's Servants, as you are ; and I tell you truly, that neither Angels, nor Prophets, nor Apoftles, nor thofe Perfons that keep the Sayings of this Book, and are fo holy as to be efteemed Saints, nor any others are to be worfhipped ; but you are to worfhip God, for he, and he only, is worthy to be the Object of your Worfhip. That the holy Angels are frequently employed in particular Miniftrations relating to Mankind, I very freely acknowledge ; but I infift upon it, that it is only from the Appointment of God : It is alfo certain from Scripture, that they are prefent at our religious Services, as St. *Paul* (d) told the

(c) Rev. xxii. 9.   (d) 1 Cor. x. 11.

Corin-

Corinthians ; and St. *Peter (e)* reprefents the Angels as defiring to look into the Myftery of our Salvation : This laft Paffage fhews their Knowlege not to be fo extenfive as to comprehend every Thing, but to be bounded ; as likewife does that other Paffage of St. *Paul* to the *Ephefians*, where he tells the *Ephefians* (f), *That the manifold Wifdom of God,* viz. the Calling of the *Gentiles, was difcovered,* or made known, *by the Church to the Principalities and Powers in heavenly Places* (that is, to the Angels). Here the Church is not faid to be taught by the Angels, but, on the contrary, that the Knowledge of the Chriftian Religion's being difcovered to the *Gentiles,* came to be known to the Angels by the Church ; as likewife that the Apoftles and Prophets (of this Church) are faid, in the fifth Verfe, to have had that Myftery (which was not made known in other Ages) now revealed unto them by the Spirit itfelf. Nor do we find that the *Jews* ever offered Prayers or Thankfgivings to the Angel that came down to the Pool of *Bethefda* (g), to render thofe Waters medicinal to the impotent People there, though by his moving or troubling the Waters, a healing Virtue was communicated to them.

But if we are not to fall down or pray to Angels, who are acknowledged to be Beings of great Honour, Power, and Might, and the conftant Attendants at the Throne of God, and fent by him on feveral Miniftrations to Mankind ;

(e) 1 Pet. i. 11, 12.   (f) Eph. iii. 6, 7, 8, 9, 10.   (g) John v. 4.

D 4   much

much lefs are we to pay that divine Honour or
Worfhip to Saints or Souls departed ; I fay, that
divine Honour or Worfhip ; for Prayers, and
Praifes, and giving of Thanks, are the moft ac-
ceptable Sacrifices, and the propereft Acts of
Adoration, that can be offered to God ; much
more than thofe of Incenfe, Sacrifice, or burnt
Offerings ; as we are told by *David* in many of
his-Pfalms (h), and that too at a Time when
thofe religious Rites and Ceremonies were offered by the pofitive Inftitution of God himfelf.
And by the Apoftle to the *Hebrews* we are commanded to offer by him (that is, by Jefus Chrift)
the (i) Sacrifice of Praife, which he calls the
Fruit of our Lips (as all Prayers are, whether
by way of Petition or Thankfgiving) in Allufion
or Appofition to the Sacrifices of the Fruits of
the Earth that were offered under the Law. Befides, the offering up our Prayers, or performing
any other Acts of religious Worfhip, to Saints or
Souls departed, is attributing to them, *firft*, The
Glory and Honour of *Ubiquity*, from their being
thereby fuppofed to hear, and be prefent to, the
Addreffes of their Supplicants in all the different
Parts of the World ; *fecondly*, Of *Omnifcience*, from
its being concluded that they know what Petitions
are made to them, by thofe who offer them the
Worfhip of the Heart, which in many Places in
Scripture is referved, and appropriated to God and
Chrift ; and *thirdly*, *Omnipotence*, from its being
believed and expected that they are able to grant
the Requefts that are fo made to them : For

(h) Pfalm l. 14, 15.   li. 15, 16.   cxli. 2.
(i) Heb. xviii. 15.

without

without all thefe Attributes are fuppofed to belong to them, it is ridiculous to put up Prayers
to Beings that cannot *hear*, or *know*, or *grant*
the Requefts that are made to them; this therefore is a natural Inference drawn from their
having Prayers made to them; I fay, that by
praying to Saints or Souls departed, we impute to them the Glory and Honour of thofe divine Attributes; and efpecially when we attribute to them the Knowledge of the Heart, which
is by the Evangelifts and Apoftles afcribed to
Chrift; and by *David* and other Prophets, in
the Old Teftament, to God; as peculiar to
them, except where by unqueftionable Revelation in Scripture we are told, That that Knowledge of the Heart has been communicated to
Mankind by God's prophetical Spirit; as in the
cafe of *Elifha* (k) with refpect to Gehazi and
Hazael; and of St. *Peter* in regard to *Annanias*
and *Saphira*; but excepting thefe Examples (and
I do not at prefent recollect any other, or if any
other can be produced in Scripture, they may be
drawn from the fame Fountain, the certain and
known Infpiration of the Holy Ghoft; I fay,
excepting thefe Examples) there are no other
Places in Scripture, where the Knowledge of the
Heart is mentioned, but what are applied to fome
one or other of the Perfons in the holy and glorious Trinity: As when St. *Paul* tells the *Romans*, That (l) *as many as are led by the Spirit of
God, are the Sons of God, whofe Spirit beareth witnefs with our Spirit*; or where our Saviour is faid

(k) 2 Kings v. 26. viii. 12. Acts v. 3, 8.
(l) Rom. viii. 14, 16.

to

to know all Men, that is, the Hearts of all Men; for he (m) *knew from the Beginning, who they were that believed not, and who should betray him*; and did not commit himself unto them, because he knew all Men.   Or, as *Moses* says to God, (n) *Let the Lord, the God of the Spirits of all Flesh,* that is, that knows the Thoughts of all Mens Hearts; or, as *David* tells his Son *Solomon,* That (o) *God searcheth all Hearts, and understandeth all Imaginations of the Thoughts*; and in the hundred and thirty-ninth Psalm, in the old Version, that (p) *God understandeth our Thoughts long before,* or as it is in the new Version, that *he understandeth our Thoughts afar off*; by which must be meant, that God knows the Thoughts of our Hearts, even before we know them ourselves; which surely will not be affirmed of any Angel, Saint, Devil, or infallible POPE! But most expressly to this Purpose is that Passage in the incomparable Prayer of *Solomon* at the Dedication of the Temple, where, speaking to God, he says, (q) *For thou, even thou only knowest the Hearts of all the Children of Men.*   Since then the Knowledge of the Heart is in Scripture only attributed to the three Persons in the glorious Trinity, as properly belonging to them, they only are worthy to have our Trust and Confidence placed in them; and to receive our Adorations, Prayers, and Thankfgivings! Whenever therefore we offer them up to any Saint or Angel, or Soul departed (who

(m) John vi. 64.   (n) Numb. xxvii. 16.
(o) 1 Chron. xxviii. 9.   (p) Psalm cxxxix. 1, 2.
(q) 1 Kings viii. 39.   2 Chron. vi. 30.

are

are all allowed to be Creatures) we place that Reliance, Truſt and Confidence in a Creature, which belongs to the Creator only ; which can- not be any Thing leſs than Idolatry.

The Excuſe that is made by moſt Papiſts for this Practice, is the ſame that was made to me by one of their Padres, when I was my ſecond Voyage in *China*, *viz.* That they pray to Saints, *&c.* only in a mediatorial Way, that they may pray to God for them ; becauſe being vile Duſt and Aſhes, and grievous Sinners, they are afraid to approach before the Throne of God without ſome Saint, *&c.* to mediate their Admiſſion, and as it were to be their Inductors ; after the Cuſ- tom practiſed here to great Princes, into whoſe Preſence no Perſons are ſo bold as to run them- ſelves without being introduced by ſome of his Courtiers : But (as I told the Padre) this is not only Will-worſhip without Warrant from Scrip- ture, but is diſhonourable to Chriſt, and expreſsly contrary to the Directions given us in the New Teſtament, to apply ourſelves to none but him, who hath told us, That (r) whoſoever cometh to him, he will in no wiſe caſt out ; and has fur- ther aſſured us, That he himſelf would go and prepare a Place for us ; and that he is not only the Truth and the Life, but alſo the Way ; and that (s) no Man cometh to the Father, but by him ; and St. *John* has told us, That when (t) *any Man ſins, we have an Advocate with the Fa- ther, Jeſus Chriſt the righteous,* who is the Pro-

(r) John vi. 37. xiv. 3. (s) John xiv. 6.
(t) 1 John ii. 1.

pitiation

pitiation for our Sins; and the Apoſtle to the *Hebrews* ſays, That (u) Chriſt was made like unto his Brethren, that he might thereby make Reconciliation for us; and thereupon adviſes and encourages us, That (x) ſeeing we have a great High Prieſt, Jeſus the Son of God, who is paſſed into the Heavens, we ſhould go boldly (not ſtay till we are introduced by ſome Saint, &c.) to the Throne of Grace, that we may obtain Mercy. And St. *Paul* has in another Place told us, That (y) becauſe or by means of Chriſt's Death he is the Mediator of the New Teſtament (or Covenant of Grace, Forgiveneſs, or Mercy) for the Redemption of the Tranſgreſſions of thoſe, who were under the Firſt Teſtament (the Covenant of Works, or Obſervance of the Law). And that Chriſt is the only Mediator between God and Man, we are further taught by the ſame St. *Paul*, in his firſt Epiſtle to *Timothy*, where he tells us, That (z) *there is one God, and one Mediator between God and Man, Chriſt Jeſus.* The Force of which Argument is, that as there is but one God, ſo there is but one Mediator, even Jeſus Chriſt; who is declared by the Author to the *Hebrews*, ſeeing he continueth ever, and and hath an unchangeable Prieſthood, to be (a) *able to ſave them to the uttermoſt that come unto God by him*, he being of ſo great Power and Dignity, that he ever liveth to make Interceſſion for us.

(u) Heb. ii. 1.　　(x) Heb. iv. 14.　　(y) Heb. lx. 15.　　(z) 1 Tim. ii. 5.　　(a) Heb. vii. 25.

The

The Doctrine of Saints departed having the Privilege of conferring or procuring Blessings for their Friends or Worshippers here on Earth, was unknown till the Popish Church (*no doubt for very wise Reasons*) declared it so to be. The Evangelists and Apostles of our Lord no where, in their Writings, attribute the least Knowledge of our Affairs to Souls departed; but direct us to pray to none but God (b) in the Name of our Lord Jesus Christ, who will send the Comforter unto us, that he may guide us into all Truth. For as for that Passage of *Dives* and *Abraham* (c), it is merely a Parable, and was not intended to be taken as a real Discourse between *Dives* in Flames, and *Abraham* in Happiness; or as designed to intimate to us, that the Souls of the Saints departed have any Knowledge of our Affairs here on Earth; but to represent to us, that after Death our Judgment, which will then be irreversible, will be according to what we have done in this Life; as also to shew us the Vanity and Folly of expecting fresh Revelations, and new Miracles, after the Neglect of those which God has been pleased to afford and make known to us in the Writings of the Old, and (to which we may now add) New Testament. And as that Doctrine was not recommended, either by our Lord, or any of his Apostles; so we may observe, that the Writings of the Old Testament are intirely free from any Hints at such a Practice, as that of addressing any Prayers to the

(b) John xv. 16. xvi. 7, 13. (c) Luke xvi. 25, 26, &c.

Patriarchs

Patriarchs or Prophets after their leaving this
World, and entering into Heaven, or into the
feparate State of Souls departed ; which we may
be the more confirmed in, from that known
Paffage of the two Prophets *Elijah* and *Elifha*,
where the former tells the latter, that (d) before
he was taken from him, he fhould afk what he
fhould do for him ; but there would have been
no Need to have confined, or pinned him down,
to what he fhould then think of afking, if *Elifha*'s praying to *Elijah*, after his Tranflation, and
being in a blifsful State, would have been a
Means to have procured him any future Bleffings
or Favours from God, or from himfelf.

From the Scriptures we learn the Place where
Chrift, our great High Prieft, is ; they declare
to us, that he (e) *is paffed into the Heavens* ; that
his Difciples faw him afcend thither ; *whom the
Heavens muft receive until the Reftitution of all
Things* ; and that he is fat down at the Right
Hand of God, *i. e.* in the higheft and moft glorious Place in Heaven.   But as for the Saints or
Souls departed, we know not where they are or
fhall be, until the general Refurrection ; for all
that we gather of them from Scripture, is, that
they are not in perfect Felicity, nor will be, till
their Souls fhall be again joined to their Bodies ;
which cannot be till the Time when our Lord
Jefus fhall come to Judgment at the laft Day ;
fo that the praying to them is abfurd, as well as
impious : Abfurd, from our Uncertainty what

(d) 2 Kings ii. 9.   (e) Heb. iv. 14.   Acts i. 9,
10.   iii. 21.   Heb. x. 12.

Condition

Condition or Place they are in ; and impious, from its being contrary to God's Command of worſhipping him ; which Command is inforced on us Chriſtians in the ſtrongeſt Manner poſſible by our Saviour, who .adds thereto the Word (f) *only,* as the true Meaning of the Extent thereof; ſaying, *Thou ſhalt worſhip the Lord. thy God, and him* ONLY *ſhalt thou ſerve* ; thereby abſolutely to reſtrain us from attributing divine Honour to any Being but God *only* ; as if he had done it pur-poſely to caution us againſt what he foreknew ſome, who pretend to be his Followers, would do in the After-ages of Chriſtianity ! As for the Saints that had been martyred, and which are repreſented in the *Revelations* as addreſſing them-ſelves to God (g) from under the Altar (that is, as I ſaid above, not in perfeČ Felicity, they be-ing to wait till their Fellow-Servants ſhould be fulfilled) though this Addreſs of theirs ſhould be allowed to have Relation to Things on the Earth, yet it ſeems rather an Imprecation and Praying for Vengeance upon their Enemies that had ſlain them, than an Interceſſion for God's Mercies upon their Friends or Followers. But ſuppoſing that Paſſage were underſtood as an Interceſſion, that God would be pleaſed to take care of thoſe that ſuffered for his Word, and for the Teſti-mony which they held ; nothing more ought to be concluded from it, than that it was a Petition for the Church in general, and not as any way interceding for any particular Perſon ; much leſs can we gather from that or any other Paſſage in

(f) Matt. iv. 10. (g) Rev. vi. 9, 10, 11.

Scripture,

Scripture, that any Patronages of particular Persons or Places are affigned to the Saints departed, as their Charge, whom, or which, they are to pray for, or watch over; and yet the *Romanifts*, as is notorioufly known, do believe particular Places and Perfons to be affigned to the Tutelage or Protection of fuch and fuch Saints, who are fuppofed to be more propitious to their Adorers and Votaries, and to have more Power to do them good at fuch and fuch Places, than at others: Witnefs the many Pilgrimages to fuch and fuch Saints, at fuch and fuch Places; the Veneration or Adoration that is paid to St. *Genevieve* at *Paris*, who is efteemed the Patronefs of that City; to St. *Michael* at *Bruffels*; St. *Mark* at *Venice*; St. *James* at *Compoftella*; and to Multitude of others at other particular Places; but above all to the Virgin *Mary*, who is efteemed the Protectrefs of a great many Places, and of almoft every particular Perfon of that Communion. What is this but Heathenifm over again? *Apollo* was worfhipped at *Delphos*, as the Virgin *Mary* is at *Loretto*; *Diana* at *Ephefus*, as St. *Winifred* is in *Wales*; and fo on *ad infinitum*. This is a Practice very much to the Difhonour of God, who can and does govern, direct, and guide, all his Creatures by his own infinite Wifdom and Power in all Places of his Dominions; and is equally mild and placable to all his Creatures, from what Places foever they addrefs him.

We do not only find from the Scriptures, that Chrift is paffed into the Heavens; but we learn from them alfo, that he there exercifes his prieftly Office of interceding for us to God the Father.

For

For they tell us, That (h) *Chrift was once offered to bear the Sins of many*; and that by that *one Offering he hath perfected for ever them that are fanctified*; that we have *Boldnefs to enter into the Holieft by his Blood*; by which *he entered once into the holy Place, having obtained eternal Redemption for us*; *who is even at the Right Hand of God, and who maketh Interceffion for us*; and appeareth in the Prefence of God for us. We have then no Need of any other Interceffors; for fince we have fuch an Advocate with the Father, as (i) *Jefus Chrift the righteous*; and that we are fure he is willing, as well as able, *to fave them to the uttermoft that come unto God by him, feeing he ever liveth to make Interceffion for them*; having himfelf told us, That (k) whatever we afk the Father in his Name, he will give it us. Let us then go directly unto God, and make our Requefts known unto him by his Son, who is the Propitiation for our Sins, and who has told us, That (l) he will refrefh all thofe that are weary, and heavy laden with the Burden of their Sins; it would be a Reflection upon our Saviour to refufe the kind Invitation he hath given us, and to addrefs ourfelves to other Mediators, whom we know nothing of. This would be a Folly equal to that of the *Jews* in the Prophet *Jeremiah*'s Time; (m) whofe Priefts knew not the Lord, and whofe Prophets prophefied by *Baal*, which he compares to the

(h) Heb. ix. 28. x. 14, 19. ix. 12. Rom. viii. 34.
(i) 1 John 2. 1.   Heb. vii. 25.   (k) John xvi. 23.
(l) Matt. xi. 28.   (m) Jerem. ii. 8.

E   forfaking

forfaking (n) the Fountain of living Water, for Cifterns that can hold no Water.

As to the Comparifon of being introduced into the Prefence of an earthly Prince, by fome of his Courtiers (as I told the Padre) nothing can be more ridiculous; for the Parallel is not juftly drawn. God and Chrift are omnifcient and omniprefent; and therefore wherever we are, we are in their Sight, and whatever we do, is known to them; fo that we can fall down before them in any Place, or at any Time; and whenever we pray to them, though it be only from the Heart, and not vocally, we are fure that our Supplications are known to them. What Need then have we to apply ourfelves to any other Introductor, but Chrift himfelf, whofe (o) Command we obey, when we pray unto God by him? But the Cafe is not the fame with refpect to thofe Petitions we may have occafion to make to earthly Princes: Thefe are finite Creatures, and circumfcribed as to Place, where we moft frequently cannot be admitted; neither can we be heard by them at all Times, by reafon of the many Avocations they have, which hinder them from giving Audience to all fuch Subjects, or others, as want to come to them. So that we are under a Neceffity of addreffing ourfelves to thofe Perfons that are about them, whenever we defire to be affifted by them, or admitted into their Prefence. However, I muft confefs, there is one Thing, wherein I think the Parallel will hold very exactly, which is, that, as when any

(n) Jerem. ii. 13.   (o) John xvi. 24.

one

one addresses himself to any great Men or Courtiers that are about the Person of an earthly Prince, he is more sedulous in paying his best Devoirs to them, and more solicitous to obtain their Favour, than that of the Prince himself; and if by that Means he obtains any Grace or Benefit, he is more truly thankful, both with Heart and Mouth, to such Courtier, than to the Prince, to whom most frequently a very superficial Thanks is returned; so I believe it is by all such Supplicants, as apply themselves to Saints or Angels to procure them any Mercies or Benefits from God; that whenever they apprehend (for I can call it nothing but apprehending that) they have been benefited by such Patrons or Patronesses, their Gratitude is exercised more towards these, their supposed, Benefactors, than it is to God himself. But the Practice of the Papists in the Invocations and Petitions, *&c.* which they put up to Angels, the Virgin *Mary,* and other Saints and Souls departed, resembles Idolatry so very much, if it do at all come short of it, that it ought to be abhorred and forsaken; if for no other Reason, yet because it is past doubt, that from the Example of the more knowing in that Church, the common People, who are Children in Understanding, offer up those Petitions and Prayers as a religious Duty, Adoration, and Service, to those Angels, Saints, and Souls departed, to whom they address themselves, with much more Earnestness and Devotion, than they do to God: Witness the Repetition of their Prayers to the Virgin and other Saints, *&c.* so much oftener than those they put

up

up to God or Chrift ; whereby the Worſhip of God and of Chrift is forced to give place to the Worſhip that is paid to his Creatures ; eſpecially to that which is paid to the Virgin *Mary*, whom they blaſphemouſly addreſs to, as a Co-ruler with her Son, or rather as a Governor or Director over him. But the Interceſſion of the Angels, Saints, *&c.* to God on their Behalf is not the only Thing the *Romaniſts* require of them ; but they rely on their Help, and formally implore their Succour, Protection, and Guidance, which they moſt earneſtly pray to them for ; and do devote themſelves to ſuch Demi-gods, of their own framing, as much at leaſt as unto God ; the doing of which is downright Idolatry.

The laſt Reaſon I ſhall give, why we are not to pray to any Angels, Patriarchs, Prophets, Saints, *&c.* for their Protection and Aſſiſtance ; or for their Interceſſion to God for us, is, that our Saviour mentions nothing of it, when he had the propereſt Opportunity imaginable to have recommended ſuch a Practice, had he thought it neceſſary or reaſonable for us to follow it ; I mean at the Time that his Diſciples deſired him to teach them how to pray ; which Requeſt of theirs he readily complied with ; by telling them in the Goſpel recorded by St. *Luke*, That when they pray, they ſhould ſay, (p) *Our Father*, &c. and in that recorded by St. *Matthew*, that they ſhould pray after this Manner, *Our Father*, &c. So that whether we uſe the very Words there ſet down, or others framed after that Form or

(p) Luke xi. 2. Matt. vi. 9.

Manner,

Manner, there is ftill no room for any Addreffes, Prayers, &c. to be made to any, but to God. only : And here we may farther obferve, that St. *Matthew* tells us, that our Saviour added a Reafon why we are thus to addrefs ourfelves to God only ; becaufe it is to God, that the Kingdom, and the Power, and the Glory do belong ; and therefore fince none of them belong to any Angels, Saints, or Souls departed, we may be fure *they* are not the proper Objects to whom our Prayers are to be addreffed ! But all thofe Tokens of Omnipotence do belong to our Saviour, and are attributed to him by St. *Jude*, when he concludes his Epiftle with a Doxology (or Form of Prayer) (q) *To the only wife God our Saviour, be Glory, Majefty, Dominion* (or Kingdom) *and Power, both now and for ever* ; where the Words (though a little tranfpofed) are the fame as thofe mentioned to belong to our Father, in the Conclufion of our Lord's Form of Prayer, as recorded by St. *Matthew.* But left it fhould be thought that this Argument, fetched from the Form of Prayer which our Lord himfelf hath taught us, proves too much, and is therefore not good, in as much as there is no Mention made therein of our Saviour, or the Holy Ghoft ; I anfwer, That the Word *Father*, ufed in this Prayer, muft not be underftood, as fpoken *perfonally*, or limited purely and fimply to God the Father, but muft be underftood to be fpoken *effentially*, as addreffed to the Trinity in Unity, who have one and the fame Effence. Had the

(q) Jude, ver. 25.

E 3 Form

Form been, O God the Father, it might have
carried with it the first Interpretation ; but as it
is said, Our Father, it will bear the latter : For
there are many Places in Scripture, where our
Creation, Preservation, and Grace (which are
the Reasons for calling God, Our Father) are
ascribed to God without the Distinction of the
Persons of the Trinity ; as where it is said of
God (spoken essentially, or without personal Distinction) That (r) he hath made us ; that we
live not by Bread alone, but by every Word that
proceedeth out of his Mouth ; that he delivers us
from Dangers ; delivers us from all Evil ; and
that in him we live, and move, and have our
Being : And the same Operations of Creation,
Preservation, and Grace, we find in other Parts
of Scripture ascribed to all the three distinct Persons in the Godhead ; as where it is said, That
(s) in the Fullness of Time God sent forth his
Son, that we might receive the Adoption of Sons ;
and our Saviour prays his holy Father not to take
his Disciples out of the World, but to preserve
them in it ; that to them that received him,
Christ gave Power to become the Sons of God ;
that by him, who is the Image of the invisible
God, and through whose Blood we have Redemption, were all Things created that are in
Heaven, and that are in Earth, visible and invisible ; and that those who are led by the Spirit

(r) Psalm c. 2, 3.　　Deut. viii. 3.　　Matt. iv. 4.
1 Sam. xvii. 37.　　2 Tim. iv. 17, 18.　　Acts xvii. 28.
(s) Gal. iv. 4, 5.　　John xvii. 11, 15. i. 12.　　Col. i.
14, 15, 16.　　Rom. viii. 14.

of

of God, are the Sons of God. By all which Means of Grace and Favour beftowed upon us by God, whether we mean according to his Effence or Perfonality, we are intitled to call him by the Appellation of *Father*; and had it been otherwife, Chrift Jefus our Saviour would no doubt have concluded the Form of Prayer that he taught us, with a Direction to have added his own Interceffion to it; or commanded us to conclude it in his Name, which he told his Difciples they fhould ufe, whenever they made their Addreffes (perfonally) to the Father; affuring them, That (t) whatever they fhould afk the Father in his Name, or for his Sake, he would give it them; and bid them afk, that they might receive.

The next Thing I fhall confider, is, the Adoration of the Hoft, or confecrated Wafer, by the Members of the Church of *Rome*; by which I believe I fhall ftill further prove them to be Idolaters, for the following Reafons.

The Hoft, or confecrated Wafer, is made of Flour, &c. which, before its Confecration by the Prieft, is by Papifts, as well as Proteftants, allowed to be only a Creature; if then, after it is confecrated, it fhould ftill remain a Creature, the adoring of it muft be downright Idolatry. But that after Confecration is does ftill remain a Wafer, or Bread, which is a Creature, the Sight, the Smell, and Tafte, do abundantly teftify; therefore thofe who adore it, are guilty of Idolatry; becaufe the giving to a Creature the

(t) John xvi. 23, 24.

E 4 Adoration

Adoration due to the Creator, is Idolatry. Again, whether it remains a Creature or a God; so long as it appears to most or all my Senses to be a Creature, I cannot positively know it to be a God; and so long as I do not positively know it to be a God, if I worship it, I am guilty of Idolatry; because God has forbidden me to worship any Thing but himself; saying, (u) *Thou shalt have no other Gods before me.* For, as in a like Case, a Man who pronounceth a Proposition, and asserts such or such a Thing to be so or so, when at that Instant of Time he is not certain, whether it is as he asserts, or not, though what he asserts may be a real Truth, yet, since he is uncertain of it, he is a Liar, and ought to be justly esteemed such; because he affirms or denies a Thing, the Truth of which he is uncertain of. So in the Case of the Host, which the *Romanists,* after Consecration, assert to be God; if they are uncertain, or in the least Doubt of its being God, though it should happen to be God, yet are they guilty of a Lie, because they are not certain of it, or are in doubt about it: And in like Manner a Communicant in that Church, who adores the Host, believing it to be God, whilst he is not certain that it is transubstantiated into the Godhead, must be guilty of Idolatry, because he pays divine Worship to that which he is not certain is God. Nor will the extravagant Evasion which is made use of in that Case, solve the Difficulty; which is, That the Person adoring does not, after the Consecration is per-

(u) Exod. xx. 3.

formed,

formed, worship the Bread, *&c.* as God or Chrift; or believe the Bread, *&c.* to be God or Chrift; but believes Chrift the fecond Perfon in the bleffed Trinity only, and not the Bread and Wine, to be there; and that that which was the Wafer or Bread, *&c.* before its Confecration, to be by that Action fo intirely changed, altered, or tranfub-ftantiated, as not to be, after that Action, there at all; but that from that Inftant, what they fee, feel, tafte, and fmell, is no longer Bread and Wine, but Chrift's natural Body and Blood; and that therefore, as their Adoration is addreffed to what they think to be Chrift, they think they are not guilty of Idolatry. But this Evafion would formerly have excufed thofe Heathens or *Jews,* whom the Prophet *Ifaiah* reproves, for falling down to the Stock of a Tree, from being Idolaters, as well as it will now the Papifts, whom we tax as Idolaters for worfhipping the Hoft, from being fo: For the Prophet does not excufe, but reproach and condemn them, when he fays, (x) He (*i. e.* the idolatrous Worfhipper) *hath formed a God, or molten a graven Image;* he *maketh it after the Figure of a Man, that it may remain in the Houfe* (or be his Houfhold God); he *maketh Part of a Tree into a graven Image; he falleth down unto it, and worfhippeth it; and prayeth unto it, and faith, Deliver me, for thou art my God.* That is, He efteemeth that Stock of a Tree, fo fet apart, or confecrated for facred Ufe, to be his God: So that their Adoration and Wor-fhip is faid by the Prophet to be addreffed to

(x) Ifaiah xliv. 10, 13, 17.

what

what they called their God ; to what they
esteemed, when set apart and consecrated to so
sacred a Purpose, to be no longer a Stock of a
Tree, but really their God : And yet we find
the Prophet taxes them with Idolatry ! without
doing them the Justice to allow of this nice Distinction, as an Extenuation or Excuse for that
heinous Sin ! But on the contrary, further up-
braids them, just as we do the Papists, for not
making use of their Reason, and the Evidence of
their Senses ; by telling them, That (y) they had
no Knowledge or Understanding, not to reflect
on the many Ways wherein the Wood of that
Tree had been used in the most common Offices
of Life ; and so little Consideration, as to make
the Residue of it a God, an Abomination ! As
if he had said,——Are you so sottish in this Matter, as to go counter to your very Senses ? Do
you not see and feel that it is Wood ? Are you
ignorant that it was carved out of the Stock of
a Tree ? Can you be so senseless then, as to
think any Part of it can be a God ? But he
gives the true Reason for this their Stupidity and
Wickedness in the next Verse, *viz.* That (z) *a
deceived Heart had turned the Idolater aside, that
he cannot deliver his Soul* (or discern the Error of
his Way) *nor say, Is there not a Lie in my Right
Hand ?* That is, That whilst their Hearts were
thus led away and deceived (whether through
Ignorance, Perverseness, or otherwise) they were
stupid enough to neglect the Use of their Reason,
and to believe contrary to the Evidence of their
Senses !

(y) Isai. xliv. 19.   (z) Isai. xliv. 20.

But

But to confider more fully the Notion of Tranfubftantiation; I think there are but two Ways, whereby to know whether a Creature can be tranfubftantiated into a God, or not. The firft is, by the natural Notions we muft have of a God, and of a Creature; and the other is, by Divine Revelation. By the natural Notions we muft have of a God, we muft conceive fuch a Being to be infinite, as to all his Attributes; to be omnifcient, omniprefent, and omnipotent, though not able to make a Contradiction; as that Good and Bad, or that Truth and Falfehood, fhould be the fame; or that a Part of any one Thing fhould be equal to, or more than, the Whole of that felf-fame individual Thing, of which it is at that Time only a Part : By the natural Notions we have of a Creature, we muft conceive it always to follow the Laws of its Creation; unlefs where thofe Laws are fet afide by the Creator's Interpofition; which being contrary to the Rules of Creation, is therfore termed miraculous. From whence it will follow, that we cannot imagine or fuppofe a folid Body can at once be, and not be; or can be in more Places than one at the fame Inftant of Time; it being the Laws of its Creation, that a folid Body fhould fubfift or exift in one Place only at one and the fame Time. That the Hoft therefore, or the Bread and Wine, fhould be tranfubftantiated into the Godhead; or into the natural Body and Blood of Chrift, and fhould be prefent in fo many different Places at once, as the Eucharift is celebrated in, is contrary to all the before-mentioned natural Notions; becaufe it is contrary

trary to the natural Notion we have of the Nature of God, and of a Creature, that a created finite Nature (as is that of Bread and Wine) fhould be converted, changed, or tranfubftantiated into an uncreated infinite Nature (as is that of God); or that the Hoft, or the Bread and Wine, and every or any Part of them, fhould be tranfubftantiated, as the Papifts affert, into the Whole of that natural *Body* and Blood of Chrift, which is united to the Godhead of the fecond Perfon in the Trinity; becaufe upon fuch a Suppofition we muft fuppofe, that there would be (in *England, France, Spain,* and the *Eaft* and *Weft Indies,* and all the World over, fuppofing in all thofe Places (which is not impoffible) the Sacrament fhould be adminiftered at the fame Time) the Whole of Chrift's natural Body and Blood, ten thoufand Times over, locally prefent in feveral Places at one and the fame Time: But it is impoffible for the Humanity, or the natural Flefh and Blood of Chrift, to be locally prefent at one and the fame Time in more Places than one; fo that if his natural Body and Blood be, as we Proteftants believe (a), locally prefent in Heaven, it cannot be, as the Papifts believe, locally prefent in fo many Places, or indeed in any one Place on Earth; and therefore it is naturally impoffible, that the Tranfubftantiation afore-mentioned fhould be effected. Further, when the Son of God, (b) *the Word, was made*

(a) Declaration at the End of the Communion-Service, in our Common Prayer-books.   (b) John i. 1, 14.

Flefh,

Flesh, and dwelt amongst us, it was not by the Conversion of one Nature into the other; but by an Union of both Natures, God and Man, into one Christ: But if every Host, or Piece of Bread, and Drop of Wine, after Consecration, has been, is, or shall be, transubstantiated into Christ, as the Papists assert, then must the Godhead of the Son (the second Person in the glorious Trinity) not only have been united (as we all believe) to the human Nature of our Lord Jesus Christ, (c) which suffered on the Cross (and which was afterwards gloriously raised from the Dead, and seen triumphantly to ascend into Heaven; where he must stay till his second Coming in the Clouds of Heaven with Power and great Glory; to be Judge of Quick and Dead) but also to all and every the Elements of Bread and Wine that have been, are, or shall be, consecrated from the Time of his Crucifixion to the End of the World, whereby they would constitute so many Christs; but this cannot be, as well from what I have already said, as because the Apostle to the *Hebrews* has told us, That Christ appeared (d) *once* (*i. e.* but once) *in the End of the World, to put away Sin by the Sacrifice of himself*; for *after he had offered that one Sacrifice for Sin, he for ever sat down at the Right Hand of God; thenceforth expecting till his Enemies be made his Footstool; for by one Offering he perfected for ever them that are sanctified;* Christ then needeth not now be offered up daily (as it is

(c) Matt. xxviii. 6. Acts i. 9. iii. 21. Matt. xxiv. 30. Acts x. 42. (d) Heb. ix. 26. x. 12, 13, 14.

pretended

pretended he is in the Sacrifice of the Mass) like those Sacrifices which were offered by the *Jewish* High Priests; who, having Infirmities, offered them up (e) *first for themselves, and then for the People*; but Christ, who was by an Oath made an High Priest, and consecrated or perfected for ever, had no Need to do this for himself; and as for his doing it for the People, he did that, *when he offered up himself* once, and thereby *perfected for ever them that are sanctified.* And yet, I say, that unless the Elements are transubstantiated, as the Papists express it, into the Divinity, as well as the Humanity or corporal Presence of Christ, the Reason they give, why they adore the Host, *viz.* because God only is there, and not the Elements of Bread and Wine, ceases.

But now comes in the Assistance of Miracles! For though this cannot be naturally affected, yet the Church of *Rome* tells us, they believe it nevertheless really performed, by the omnipotent Power of God; which they think they are sufficiently authorised to believe, both can and does effect it, from what the Scripture (which both they and we acknowledge to be a Divine Revelation) declares concerning this Matter; where our Saviour, the Word and Son of God, says, That the Bread and Wine is his Body and Blood; and therefore, since he who was Truth itself, has said, That it is his Body and Blood, it must most certainly be so; and from thence they believe, that what could not be done according to

(e) Heb. vii. 27. 21, 28. 27. x. 24.

the

the Nature of Things, was, and is, and may be, brought about by the miraculous and over-ruling Power of the God of Nature. To which I answer, That the Scripture is most certainly a Divine Revelation, and therefore that all the Declarations therein made are undoubtedly true! If then it be declared in Scripture, that the Bread and Wine which our Saviour at the Institution of the Sacrament took, brake, and gave to his Disciples; and which was taken, eaten, and drank by them in his Presence, was really the very natural Body and Blood of him, who was then lying or sitting by them at the Table, alive, unbroken, and uncrucified; and who was at the same Time speaking to them; and that those Words, *This is my Body, and this is my Blood*, were spoken in a literal, and not in a figurative Sense; and were intended to be understood in a natural, and not with an allegorical or metaphocal Meaning; then indeed it must be true, that it was his very natural Body and Blood, which was then swallowed down their Throats into their Stomachs, while he was yet, and for some Time after, at the Table preaching to them that Divine Sermon contained in the thirteenth, fourteenth, fifteenth, sixteenth and seventeenth Chapters of St. *John*'s Gospel; and who some Time after went to *Gethsemane*, and was there in Person arrested by the Officers of the High Priest, and afterwards crucified, and put to the most exquisite Torments, and the most shameful and ignominious Death; whilst those other Parts, or Wholes, of him that the Disciples had eaten and drank, were intirely safe, free from Tortures, and

and out of Harm's Way; being run away with,
when his Difciples forfook him and fled! But
to be ferious; if it be not true from Scripture,
that his Words are to be taken in a literal Senfe
according to the Popifh Explanation of them,
then it is not true, that the Bread and Wine
which he took into his Hands, and delivered to
his Difciples, to be by them taken, eaten, and
drank, were tranfubftantiated into the very natural Body and Blood of him, who fo took and
delivered them; and confequently, that in Reality
the Elements or Subftance of Bread and Wine
did ftill remain in their true and natural State,
after he had bleffed or confecrated them to the
fpiritual Ufe and Benefit of his Difciples, who
(f) were often to eat and drink the facramental
Bread and Wine in Remembrance of his moft
exalted Love in dying for them and for all Mankind. And if this can be proved, it will follow,
that fince the Elements that were bleffed or confecrated by our Saviour himfelf, who was con-
feffedly God, and had an omnipotent Power to
do whatever he pleafed, or thought neceffary,
(Contradictions as before-mentioned excepted)
did, after they were fo bleffed or confecrated,
ftill remain Bread and Wine in their natural
State; I fay, it will follow, that no other fub-
fequent Confecration, by any Chriftian Prieft or
Minifter whatfoever, can tranfubftantiate them
into Chrift; becaufe no Confecration can be
more operative than that of our Saviour himfelf; for what he faid in another Cafe, will cer-

(f) Luke xxii. 19, 20.   1 Cor. xi. 24, 25.

tainly

tainly hold as good in this, that (g) *he that is sent is not greater than he that sent him* ; from whence we may be affured, that no Prieft or Minifter of the Chriftian Religion can perform greater Miracles than the Author thereof. And therefore (whatever the Communicant may think) he that adores thofe Symbols or outward Signs, is guilty of Idolatry, becaufe he adores that which ftill remains a Creature, notwithftanding its Confecration. It remains then, that I prove that the Words of the Inftitution were not fpoken in a literal, but in a figurative Senfe ; not according to the Popifh, but according to the Proteftant Explanation of them ! which I fhall do, by obferving, *firft*, That our Saviour's Manner of fpeaking was always extremely elegant and rhetorical ; and filled with all the Figures ufually practifed by the moft learned Perfons ; a Thing obferved of him by the *Jews*, who being amazed at the Eloquence and Force of his Doctrine, and the mighty Energy of his Divine Difcourfes, cried out, How knoweth this Man Letters, having never learnt ? So that it is no Wonder to find him making ufe, at that Time, of a figurative Expreffion, which was a Thing he fo commonly practifed in his general Difcourfes. And, *fecondly*, that when he had any Thing extraordinary to inculcate upon the Minds of his Difciples, which he intended they fhould take the greater Notice of ; it was ufual for him to make ufe of fuch figurative Expreffions, as could not but excite their Attention the more to what

(g) John xiii. 16.

F

he

he had a mind fhould remain in their Thoughts. As when he was defirous, of informing them, that there was no Way of coming to God, but by him ; he tells them, He is the Door ; the good Shepherd ; that it is· he that leads and fecures, and lays down his Life for, his Sheep ; *i. e.* that it is by him alone, and by his Merits and Interceffion (not by the pretended Merits and Interceffion of others, who are Hirelings) that God will be reconciled to us. Not that he defired they fhould believe from thofe Words, that he was tranfubftantiated into a material Door, and turned upon Hinges ; or that he was literally a Shepherd, who had animal Sheep under his Care; but they were metaphorical Expreffions, which he made ufe of to reprefent to them, that as in this Life, or the natural State of Things here; the good Shepherd takes care of his Sheep, that he may fecure them from Danger, and lead them through the Door into the Sheepfold ; fo in refpect to the Life eternal, or the State of Grace and Mercy, we muft be conducted by him, and by him only, to the heavenly Kingdom of his Father. Again, when he would reprefent to them the Neceffity there was, that his Followers fhould conftantly abide in the Doctrine of his Religion, and not forfake it ; he reprefents himfelf to them under the Image or Similitude of a Vine, and his Difciples under that of the Branches ; where, as in the other Inftances already given, he ufes the fame pofitive, though figurative, Manner of fpeaking, faying, (h) *I am the true*

(h) John xv. 1, 4, 5.

Vine,

Vine, and my Father is the Husbandman ; and that as the Branches cannot bear Fruit of themselves, except they abide in the Vine ; so neither could they, except they continued in him. The Words, *I am the Vine* ; *my Father is the Husbandman* ; and *ye are the Branches* ; are certainly figurative Expressions ; but not more so, than those others ; *This is my Body, this is my Blood* ; which are spoken by the same Person, during the same long Discourse recorded by St. *John* (i), when our Saviour celebrated the Passover in Remembrance of the Deliverance of the *Israelites* from their temporal Bondage in *Egypt* ; and when he instituted the Sacrament, or euchariftical Feaft, in Remembrance of his own Death, which he was then just going to suffer for our Deliverance from the spiritual Bondage of Sin : And therefore, as the former Expressions were never intended to be understood in a literal, but in a metaphorical or allegorical Sense, so these laft ought to be understood in the like Manner ; *viz.* That as the vital Heat and Moifture of our human Bodies are procured, nourifhed, and invigorated by the Suftenance received from the Creatures of Bread and Wine ; so our spiritual Souls are preserved from Sin, fanctified to perform virtuous Actions, and ftrengthened to refift Temptations, from the Communication of the (k) Body and Blood of Chrift (not corporeally, but) spiritually (and therefore verily and indeed) taken and received by the Faithful in the Lord's Supper. For there

(i) John xiii. 14, 15, 16, 17.   (k) Laft Answer but two in the Catechifm of the Church of *England.*

can

can be no Reafon affigned, why his Difciples were to believe one Part of our Saviour's Difcourfe, that contradicted the Evidence of their Senfes; as that he was a Door, a Vine, &c. when at the fame Time they faw, and heard him walk and fpeak, fhould be fpoken in a figurative Senfe; and yet that another Part of the fame Difcourfe, which equally contradicted the Evidence of their Senfes; as that the Bread and Wine was his Body and Blood, when at the fame Time they faw him perform the fame Functions of natural Life, as in the former Cafe, fhould be fpoken in a literal Senfe: I fay, there can be no Reafon for the different Acceptation of the Phrafes, unlefs it fhould arife from the Scope and Intention of his Difcourfe, or the Defign of the Inftitution itfelf. But the Scope and Intention of his Difcourfe, and the Defign of the Inftitution, will be no Help to them in this Matter; for thofe I think were plainly thus: Our Saviour, after having lived here on Earth a fufficient Space of Time, during which he had led a holy, virtuous, meek, and charitable Life; that fo by his Example, as well as by the Doctrines and Precepts he taught, he might fhew his Difciples, that they ought to follow the Example he had fet them, as well as to conform their Belief and Practice to the Rules he had given them to walk by; and being now about to perform the laft Scene of his great Love, the dying for them and all Mankind; by which Sacrifice, or Offering of himfelf, he was fully to fatisfy and appeafe the offended Juftice of his Father, and remove his Anger from us: And having told them, That

he

he would intercede for them in thofe heavenly Manfions whither he was going, and that he (l) would there prepare a Place for them, that where he fhould be, they might be alfo; as likewife, that he would fend them another Comforter (m), even the Holy Ghoft, who fhould lead them into all Truth; and confer the Graces of Sanctification, not only upon them, but alfo upon all (n) thofe who fhould believe on him through their Word: And well knowing how apt Mankind is to forget their beft Friends and greateft Benefactors; he thought fit, under the Chriftian Difpenfation, to appoint a holy and folemn Memorial of this his wondrous and ineftimable Love, which fhould have Continuance as long as the Gofpel fhould be profeffed throughout the World, left we fhould forget the great Things which he had done and fuffered for us; and therefore inftituted this facred Feaft, as a perpetual Ordinance, to be often celebrated in Memory of his moft painful, but meritorious Death, which he was juft going to fuffer in our ftead, and for the Expiation of our Sins, that he might free us from the Death of Sin, and raife us to Newnefs of Life. And this he did in Allufion and Conformity to that Feaft of the Sacrifice of the Pafcal Lamb amongft the *Jews*, which that People were commanded to celebrate, in Remembrance and Acknowledgment of the great Goodnefs of God in freeing them from their temporal Bondage in *Egypt*, and in conducting them to the

(l) John xiv. 2, 3.   (m) John xvi. 7, 13.
(n) John xvii. 17, 20.

           Land

Land of *Canaan*; which was the exact Type of our Saviour, who was to free us by his Death from the spiritual Bondage of our Sins, and afterwards exalt us into the happy Manfions of Glory. Thus, by the Analogy or Likeness between the Type and the Antitype, it appears (as well as from the other Reasons I have already given, and shall further give) that the Intention of our Lord (when he instituted this sacramental, *i. e.* mysterious Feast) was only, that we should thereby (n) continue a perpetual Memory of that his precious Death, until his coming again; and therefore, when he (o) took the *Bread, and blessed it*; and afterwards *the Cup, and gave Thanks*; he did not transubstantiate the Bread and Wine into his Body and Blood, by his calling them such; but only thereby consecrate and sanctify the Bread and Wine to a spiritual Use, *for the Remission of the Sins of many*; which Benefit was obtained for us by the offering up of Christ, whose Life was given (p) as a Ransom for, and to bear the Sins of many: For like as at his Baptism in the River *Jordan* he had sanctified Water, to the mystical washing away of Sin, that as our Bodies were washed with pure Water, our Hearts might be sprinkled from an evil Conscience; so at his laying down his Life on Mount *Calvary*, he sanctified Bread and Wine to the mystical taking away of Sin, that as our Bodies are nourished by Bread and Wine, our

(n) Prayer of Confecration. *English* Liturgy.
(o) Matt. xxvi. 26, 27, 28.   (p) Matt. xx. 28,
Heb. ix. 28.   x. 22.

Con=

Confciences, (q) by the Offering of the unfpot-
ted and unpolluted Body and Blood of Chrift,
might be *purged from dead Works to ferve the
living God.*

Our bleffed Saviour does indeed tell his Difciples, That (r) that Bread and that Cup were
his Body and his Blood, which were given and
fhed for them and for many, which they fhould
eat and drink in Remembrance of him. The
true Meaning of which Words, according to the
Interpretation given of them by St. *Paul* to the
Corinthians, which he fays he delivered them as
he had received it from the Lord, I take to be
no other than this; That as often as they fhould
eat that Bread, and drink that Cup, they fhould
fhew the (s) Lord's Death till he come ; that *is,*
they would thereby exprefs the grateful Senfe
they had of his ineftimable Love in dying for
them, and in undergoing in their ftead the Wrath
of his heavenly Father, in order to procure for
them, and for many, the Remiffion of Sins :
That this Remembrance of our Saviour's Paffion
was to be continued till his coming again, that
is, that it was not defigned for the Apoftles alone,
but for all the Faithful that fhould believe on him
through their Word, to the End of the World
(the Time of his coming again) who muft fhew
this Remembrance of him, by drinking as well
as eating (contrary to the Practice of the Church
of *Rome,* where fome only do both, and fome
only eat) thefe Symbols of his Death, and Pledge

(q) Heb. ix. 14.   (r) Mark xiv. 24. Luke xxii.
19, 20.   (s) 1 Cor. xi. 23, 24, 25, 26.

F 4   of

of his Love. This is all that is said by our Saviour himself at the Time of his instituting this Sacrament; or by St. *Paul*, when he explained it to the *Corinthians*, who was, we are sure, divinely inspired, and therefore must be the best Expositor: And seeing that all Scripture is written by the Inspiration of God, and is able to make us wise unto Salvation, *i. e.* that all Things necessary for us to know, in order to our Salvation, are contained therein; I dare not add any thereto, any more than I dare diminish therefrom; nor make any Explanation of any Part of them, that shall be contrary to any other Part of them; believing that the same Woes, which were threatened should befal the Children of *Israel*, (t) if they should add to, or diminish from, what was delivered them in the Law of *Moses*; or were denounced against such Persons as should add to, or diminish from, the Prophecies contained in the *Revelations* of St. *John*; shall surely attend such Christians, as shall wilfully and knowingly falsify the Scriptures delivered to them by the Evangelists and Apostles of our Lord. And therefore, since there is nothing to be discovered in the holy Scriptures, either from the Scope of our Saviour's Discourse, or the Design of his Institution, but only the perpetuating to the End of the World the Memory of our Saviour's wondrous Love and meritorious Death, and the inestimable Benefits which Christians were to reap from it: As the Pardon of their Sins; the Gift of the Holy Ghost to sanctify them anew; and

(t) Deut. iv. 2. Rev. xxii. 18, 19.

the

the being made Heirs of an Inheritance incorruptible in the Heavens; all which our Saviour procured for us by his suffering in our stead, by whose Stripes we were healed, when he was made an Offering for Sin, and that he bear our Sins in his own Body on the Tree; there ought to be no other Meaning fixed thereon, than that metaphorical or allegorical Sense I have already mentioned. Which is the rather to be believed, since it will thereby, as is already hinted, agree the more exactly with the other Sacrament, that of Baptism; which was instituted by our Saviour for the taking away of original Sin, as well as of such other Sins as had been committed by the Converts to the Christian Religion before their being baptized into it: For, as in the Sacrament of Baptism, Water is sanctified to the washing away of Sin; not from our being materially or formally washed with it, which is only (u) *the putting away of the Filth of the Flesh*; but by the Answer of a good Conscience, from the spiritual Life that is conferred on us by the Resurrection of Christ from the Dead: So, in the Sacrament of our Lord's Supper, the Bread and Wine are sanctified to the Remission of our Sins after Baptism; not from our materially or formally receiving that very Body and Blood of Christ, which was crucified; but from our spiritually feeding on his most precious Body and Blood, through Faith in his Death, (x) *who gave himself for us, that he might redeem us from all Iniquity.*

(u) 1 Pet. iii. 21.　　　(x) Titus ii. 14.

Having

Having thus shewn you that our Saviour's
Words, at the Time of his instituting the Sacra—
ment, were not spoken in a literal Sense, as the
Papists say they were, when they maintain the
Doctrine of Transubstantiation ; I shall now go
on to shew you, that they were spoken in a
figurative Sense, according to the Doctrine of
Protestants, by whom Transubstantiation is de—
nied to be true ; which I shall do from several
Passages in Scripture, but more especially from
the Discourse of our blessed Lord to the *Jews*,
as recorded by St. *John* in the sixth Chapter of
his Gospel ; which may well be taken as an
Explanation given by our Saviour himself of that
holy Feast, which he intended afterwards to in—
stitute as a Memorial of his Passion and Death,
to all succeeding Ages, to be observed and kept
by his Followers, as the characteristical Mark of
Christianity.   In that Discourse (y) he reproves
all such *Hearers of his Word,* as flocked after him
from any other Consideration than that of a spi—
ritual Life ; and, upon the Demand which the
Jews made him, that *he would shew them a Sign
of his Mission*, like that of *Moses*, who gave
their Fathers Manna from Heaven, he tells them,
*he was the Bread of Life, which was given them
by God from Heaven, to give Life to the World* ;
which the *Jews* taking in a literal Sense, were
offended at, alleding, *that they knew his Father
and Mother*, and that therefore *that could not be* ;
to which he answers, *That the Manna was but a
Type of him, which their Fathers eat in the Wilder-*

(y) John vi. 26, 27, 31, 33, 35, 41, 42, 51.

ness,

ness, and died after it ; but that *he was the living Bread, that came down from Heaven, which, if any Man eat of, he should live for ever ;* and then expressly tells them, *That the Bread he would give them was his Flesh, which he would give for the Life of the World.* , But, that those who should eat his Flesh should live for ever, we are sure could not be true, if it was meant in a literal Sense ; for his Apostles all of them eat and drank his real and natural Flesh and Blood (if so be that the Bread and Wine which he blessed and gave to them, and which they accordingly eat and drank at the Time of his instituting the Sacrament, and which he called his Body and Blood, was thereby transubstantiated into his real and natural Body and Blood) and yet they are all of them long since dead and rotten ! So that, in order that our Saviour's Words may be consistent with Truth, we must of Necessity understand them in a figurative Sense ; which is what our Lord himself has taught us to do : For, upon the gross Misapprehension which the *Jews* had conceived of those Words, when they strove (or disputed) among themselves, saying (z), *How can this Man give us his Flesh to eat ?* thinking that he meant his natural Flesh and Blood, he declared, *That though his Flesh was Meat indeed, and his Blood was Drink indeed,* and that *He who should eat his Flesh, and drink his Blood, should dwell in him, and he in them ;* and that, *as he lived by the Father, so they should live by him ;* yet he acquaints his Disciples, who murmured (or

(z) John vi. 52, 55, 56, 57, 63.

were

were diſſatisfied) at theſe Expreſſions (in order to reclaim them from their Miſtake, and to give them a right Underſtanding of his Words) *that the Words which he then ſpake, they were Spirit and they were Life*; that is, they were not to be underſtood, as they erroneouſly had conceived them, to have a groſs and carnal Meaning, but were to be taken to have a ſpiritual and figurative Meaning: Like that other memorable Saying of his to the Woman of *Samaria*, when he told her, that (a) *whoſoever ſhould drink of the* (material) *Water of* Jacob's *Well, ſhould thirſt again; but that whoever ſhould drink of the Living Water that he ſhould give them, ſhould never thirſt; but it ſhould be in them a Well of Water ſpringing up unto everlaſting Life*: By which was to be underſtood his Doctrine, according to which his Followers were to worſhip God in Spirit and in Truth; agreeably to the Nature of God, who is a Spirit, and therefore ought to be worſhipped in that Manner.

Again; when upon the Diſpute that was at *Antioch*, between ſuch *Jewiſh* Chriſtians as were zealous for keeping the Law of *Moſes*, and the *Gentile* Chriſtians, who did not think themſelves bound by it (b), and were therefore neither circumciſed, nor would keep the *Levitical* Law, in obſerving the Difference between one Sort of Meat from another; the Thing came to be referred to the Deciſion of the Apoſtles and Elders at *Jeruſalem*, in the Firſt Chriſtian Council, whereof St. *James* the Apoſtle was Prolocu-

(a) John iv. 13, 14.   (b) Acts xv. 5.

tor;

tor ; they came to this Determination, That although the Law of *Moses* was not to be obligatory upon Chriſtians, yet that it was neverthelefs incumbent upon them to abſtain from Four Things forbidden by that Law *(c)* ; the Two firſt, *viz.* Fornication and Pollution of Idols (or Meats offered to them) becaufe they were real Sins ; the Two laſt, *viz.* from Blood, and from Things ſtrangled (whereby the Blood was left in them) ; becaufe the eating fuch Things might give Offence to the *Jews*, who had the eating of Blood in fuch Abhorrence, that, fhould the Chriſtians avowedly eat thereof, it might probably be a Means to prevent the *Jews* from embracing the Chriſtian Religion : But, had our Saviour ordained, at the inſtituting his Sacrament, that his natural Body and Blood fhould be eaten and drank in the Sacrament, it had not been in the Power of St. *James*, and the reſt of that Council, who were all, or moſt of them, the cotemporary Difciples, and many of them the Apoſtles, of our Lord ; and muſt therefore be perfectly well acquainted with the Nature of the Sacrament, and the Deſign of our bleſſed Lord in the inſtituting of it : I fay, it had not been in their Power, let the Conſideration be never fo plaufible, to have temporifed in this Cafe, or to have put a Glofs on a Matter of fo extraordinary a Nature, if they had really underſtood our Saviour to have fpoken thofe Words in a literal Senfe ; but, on the contrary, they would have been obliged to have laid hold of that Opportunity openly and plainly to

(c) Acts xv. 20, 29.

have

have avowed their eating of Blood ; and, inftead of recommending to the Chriftians of *Antioch* the abftaining from it, to have commanded them to eat and drink it as often as they fhould celebrate the Lord's Supper, as a caracteriftical Mark of their being the Difciples of our Lord, who had enjoined his Followers fo to do.

Another Thing to be obferved is, the Manner of Expreffion made ufe of both by our Saviour and St. *Paul.* Our Saviour at the Inftitution, as all the Three Evangelifts, St. *Matthew,* St. *Mark,* and St. *Luke* (d), that mention this Matter, tell us, *took the Cup, and when he had given Thanks, he faid unto them, This Cup is my Blood of the New Teftament, which is fhed for many for the Remiffion of Sins* (e) ; which is itfelf a direct figurative Expreffion ; the Word *Cup* being made ufe of by way of Trope (a Figure in Rhetorick) to fignify the Wine that was in the Cup ; as that Wine was to fignify the Blood that our Saviour was to fhed : This is plain from the next Verfe, where he fays (f), *I will not drink henceforth of this Fruit of the Vine, until,* &c. So that after he had taken the Cup, and given Thanks, and given it to them to drink of, calling it his Blood of the New Teftament, he ftill calls it, *This Fruit of the Vine.* From whence nothing can be plainer, than that it remained the Fruit of the Vine, or Wine, after he had confecrated it ; and that therefore it was not tranfubftantiated into

(d) Matt. xxvi. 27, 28. Mark xiv. 23, 24. Luke xxii. 20. (e) Matt. xxvi. 28. (e) Ibid. ver. 29.

his

his Blood : But thofe Words muft be underftood to have been fpoken with Reference or Allufion, from the natural Effect which their partaking of the material Food of Bread and Wine fhould have upon their Bodies, to the fpiritual Effect which fhould be wrought upon their Souls, by their fpiritually participating of his Body and Blood, when they fhould pioufly and thankfully celebrate this facred Feaft, according to his own Inftitution, in Memory of his great Love in laying down his Life in fo bitter a Manner, to reconcile them to God. St. *Paul* alfo ufes the fame Expreffion in the xith Chapter of his Firft Epiftle to the *Corinthians* (g), where, after he had told them in the 23d Verfe, *that Jefus took Bread,* and in the 24th Verfe called it *his Body,* and in the 25th Verfe, *that he took the Cup, and* faid, *This Cup is the New Teftament in my Blood,* he ftill goes on, and terms them *Bread* and *Cup* in the Three following Verfes ; by which it is manifeft, that he efteemed it to be ftill Bread and Wine, after it had been bleffed or confecrated by our Saviour. Befides, it was the common and accepted Notion of the primitive Church, under the Miniftration of the Apoftles themfelves, that it was Bread, *&c.* as we may fee by feveral Places in the *Acts of the Holy Apoftles* ; where, whenever there is any mention made of their receiving this Sacrament at the Times of their meeting together for publick and folemn Worfhip, it is always expreffed by the Words, *Break-*

(g) 1 Cor. xi. 23, 24, 25, 26, 27, 28.

ing

ing of Bread (i).   As likewise when St. *Paul* reproves the Corinthians, for the diforderly and finful Manner in which they came to receive this
Sacrament, he conftantly calls it *Bread*, &c.   He
tells them, (k) *That, fince as often as they did eat
that Bread, and drink of that Cup, they did fhew
forth* (make manifeft their Remembrance of) *the
Lord's Death*, they were not to participate thereof
in an irreverent Manner ; or *to eat that Bread,
and drink that Cup of the Lord unworthily* (l), as
their Practice then was ; for whofoever fhould
do fo, ought to be efteemed guilty of a very great
Affront and Indignity offered to the Body and
Blood of our Lord, reprefented and participated
by thofe Signs or Symbols ; fo that whofoever
fhould eat of that Bread, and drink of that Cup,
without examining (or ferioufly confidering with)
himfelf, what he was about to do, might well
be faid *to eat and drink the fame unworthily* ; and
thereby be juftly liable to be punifhed with Sicknefs, Pain, and Death (which is the true Meaning of the Words, *eating and drinking Damnation to themfelves*, as ufed in that Place) becaufe
they did not difcern the Lord's Body, *i. e.* They
did not confider, that, although the earthly or
elementary Subftance of Bread and Wine remained the fame as it was before, yet feeing it
was fet apart, or confecrated, to fo facred a Purpofe as that of reprefenting the Death of Chrift,
and of communicating to them the Benefits, and
bleffed Effects, of our Saviour's Sacrifice of his

(i) Acts ii. 42, 46.   xx. 7.   (k) 1 Cor. xi. 26,
(l) 1 Cor. xi. 29.

                                        Body

Body broken, and his Blood fhed for them ; and of being vifible Memorials of his dying Love ; they ought to be received with a Reverence fuitable to fo facred an Appointment : The want of which Confideration, and the brutifh and finful Manner in which they had hitherto received it, was the Occafion (m) that fo many of them had been vifited with *Weaknefs,* and *Sicknefs,* and even with *Death itfelf.* But there is a further Ufe that I muft not forget to make of this Paffage of Scripture, *viz.* That it is plain from hence, that the *Corinthians* were fo far from believing, that the Elements of Bread and Wine, when bleffed or confecrated by their Paftors, whether Apoftles or others in that primitive Age of the Church, were tranfubftantiated into the Body and Blood of Chrift, or from having them in fo high a Veneration as to adore them, that they were, on the contrary, guilty of a moft enormous Crime, from the Want of a due Reverence for them. Had the Church of *Corinth* believed, that the Elements of Bread and Wine in the Sacrament were tranfubftantiated into the Body and Blood of Chrift, they would not furely have ftood in need of the Reproof of St. *Paul,* admonifhing them to participate thereof with a befitting Reverence ; they would not, in that Cafe, have come to it either drunken, or otherwife difordered, had thofe who converted them to Chriftianity taught them what the Romanifts pretend to be the Truth of the Cafe, That the Bread and Wine is changed, or tranfubftantiated,

(m) 1 Cor. xi. 20, 21, 22, 30.

G into

into the Body and Blood of Chrift.   And here I cannot but obferve, that although they were guilty of this great Offence, yet the Apoftle, to cure them of it, does not tell them, that they were guilty of the higheft Sin imaginable, by coming in a drunken and diforderly Manner to eat and drink God himfelf (as it would have been had it been really fo); or that tho' they thought they received only Bread and Wine, yet that in Truth they were widely miftaken, for there was no Bread and Wine there, fince what they received was really the very Flefh and Blood of God our Saviour.   This, no doubt, would have been what St. *Paul* would have told them, had he been of the fame Opinion that the Church of *Rome* is now of.   No; inftead of that he tells them, over and over again, that what they received was *Bread and Wine* only, fet apart to a divine and fpiritual Ufe; which, therefore, they ought to receive with due Examination, Difcernment, or Confideration; but he does not fay with *Adoration*; which, if he had thought they ought to have done, he would doubtlefs have told them fo, which would have been the moft effectual Way in the World to have convinced them of the Wickednefs of their former brutifh and irreverent Practice, and to have prevented their relapfing into the like finful Courfe for the future.

To fhew you further that it is not of Neceffity to be underftood, that by the Expreffions, *This Bread is my Body*, or *This Cup* or *Wine is my Blood*, is meant, that the Things are really what they are faid to be; but only that they
signify

fignify (are a Sign, a Type, or Symbol of) what they are faid to be ; that is, that this Bread fig- nifies my Body, this Cup fignifies my Blood of the New Teftament ; I fhall alledge fome paral- lel Expreffions in Scripture very appofite to this Cafe : As that in the xxiiid Chapter of the 2d Book of *Samuel* (n), where *David* refufes to drink of the Water of *Bethlehem*, that was brought him by Three of his mighty Men, faying, *Is not this the Blood of the Men that went in Jeo- pardy of their Lives ?* Not that he thought it was their Blood, for he faw and knew it was Water ; but that if he fhould drink that Water, which they brake through the Enemies Camp to fetch him, it would be as if he fhould drink fo much of their Blood, which they had expofed to fetch him that Water. Again ; although the Hair of the Head and Beard, which the Prophet *Ezekiel* was commanded by God Almighty to fhave off, to burn, to fmite with a Knife, to fcatter, and to bind up in his Skirts, is faid in as pofitive a Manner of Expreffion to be *Jerufalem* (o), as that where it is faid, *This Bread is my Body,* &c. faying, *This is* Jerufalem ; yet no more was there- by intended, than only the prefiguring and re- prefenting that under the Expreffions of fuch and fuch Things which were to be done to the Hair, fhould be underftood, that the Judgments of Difperfion and the Sword fhould befal that City, and the Inhabitants thereof. And in the New Teftament St. *Paul* tells the *Corinthians* (p), that

(n) 2 Sam. xxiii. 17.   (o) Ezekiel v. 5.
(p) 1 Cor. x. 4.

the

the Children of Ifrael *in the Wildernefs drank of the fpiritual Rock which followed them, and that Rock was Chrift* ; where it is to be remarked, that the Rock in *Horeb* is faid pofitively to be Chrift ; and might, no doubt, with as much Propriety be faid to be as truly and really Chrift, though he was not born till many Generations after the Children of *Ifrael* came into the Land of *Canaan*, as the Bread and Wine might be faid to be his Body and Blood, who was then living, and was not crucified till the Day after he had pronounced thofe Words. Further ; the Children of *Ifrael* are faid to *drink of the Rock* ; where the Rock is by a Trope put for the Waters that flowed or gufhed out of it, and followed them in their Journeyings through the Wildernefs ; in like Manner as the Cup is put for the Wine that was in it. But the more exprefsly to fhew the exact Refemblance of this Type to Chrift, who is *a Well of living Water* (q), St. *Paul* tells the *Corinthians*, that the Children of *Ifrael* drank of the *fpiritual Rock* (r) that followed them, which Rock was Chrift ; thereby alluding to the fpiritual Effufion of the Holy Ghoft, that fhould be beftowed on fuch Communicants as, with a true, penitent, and lively Faith, *fhould fpiritually eat the Flefh of Chrift, and drink his Blood* (s).

From all which Paffages out of the Books of *Mofes* and the Prophets, or the Difcourfes of our Saviour, and the Writings of his Apoftles, it is abundantly evident, that nothing can be gathered

(q) John iv. 14.　　(r) 1 Cor. x. 4.　　(s) Exhortation in the Communion Service.

to

to support the Notion of Transubstantiation, by any Declarations or Expressions in either the Old or New Testament ; which are the only divine Revelations that we can possibly depend upon.

As to what is said by our Adversaries of the *Romish* Communion, That the greater the Difficulty of believing any Doctrine is, the greater is the Faith of those who believe it ; and therefore, that their Faith who believe the Doctrine of Transubstantiation is much greater, and more meritorious, than any we can pretend to, who refuse to believe Things contrary to our Senses : I answer, That the Persuasion of the Papists, as to this Point, is not Faith, but a stupid Credulity. *Faith* is described, by the Apostle to the *Hebrews* (t), to be, *the Substance* (Ground, Confidence, or Assurance) *of Things hoped for, the Evidence of Things not seen :* It is not said to be the Evidence of Things contrary to what is seen, there being a very wide Difference between believing, as the Patriarchs (whose Praises are celebrated in that Chapter) did, Things that were, by some Way or other, divinely revealed to them should certainly come to pass, though they did not then see them, or know how, or when, they should happen (which was, therefore, the Ground of their Hope and Faith) : I say, there is a very wide Difference between this, and the believing Things contrary to what they saw or felt, *&c.* which would be believing Things contrary to the Evidence of their Senses ; whereas the Evidence of our Senses is as much a Principle implanted

(t) Heb. xi. 1.

G 3

in

in us by God, to guide us with relation to fuch
Things as are the Objects of our Senfes, as our
Faith is with relation to fuch Things as are divinely, or otherwife, revealed to us. Neither is
Faith, or Belief, a Principle abfolutely in our
Power, which we can take up, or lay down, as
we pleafe; for we cannot, though we would
never fo fain, really and truly believe Contradiction; we cannot, it is not in our Nature to,
believe Impoffibilities. But, fay the *Romanifts,*
we do not pretend that this Tranfubftantiation
is poffible any otherwife to be effected than by
Miracle; and as God can, and often does, work
Miracles, fo he may caufe this Change to be miraculoufly performed, and therefore it may be
believed: To which I anfwer, It is very true,
that God can, and often does, work Miracles;
but then it is abfolutely impoffible for Mankind
to believe any Thing to be a Miracle, unlefs their
Senfes (which are the only Means they have
whereby to judge of a Miracle) tells them that
it is one: For, though the Scripture, which is a
divine Revelation, tells them, that Miracles are,
and may be, wrought by the Power of God,
yet, whenever there is any one individual Miracle wrought, Mankind cannot believe, or even
fo much as know, any Thing of it, unlefs the
Judgment of their Senfes affure them of it. All
the Miracles of *Mofes,* and of our Saviour, were
evidently, though miraculoufly, wrought; fo
that the People, before whom they were wrought,
were plainly fenfible they were Miracles, from
the Affurance given them thereof by their Senfes
of Feeling or Seeing, &c. The miraculous Plagues
brought

brought upon the *Egyptians* were to be seen and felt ; the Paffage of the Children of *Ifrael* through the *Red Sea*, and their being fupplied with Quails and Manna in the Wildernefs ; the flowing of the Water out of the Rock in *Horeb* ; were all vifibly miraculous, and above the Power of Nature. Our Saviour's feeding the Multitude with only Five Loaves and Two Fifhes, was a Miracle fo vifible and obvious to their Senfes, that they immediately faid, (u) *This is of a Truth that Prophet that fhould come into the World.* Here the People, who faw there were but Five Loaves and Two Fifhes, the Species whereof they vifibly faw, fo multiplied as to fatisfy the Hunger of fo many thoufand Perfons as actually and evidently eat thereof, immediately believed that it was done by a divine Power, and thereupon profeffed their Faith in him, by faying, *That he was* (the true Meffiah, or) *that Prophet that fhould come into the World* ; and were thereupon going by Force to make him a King : And, when he turned the Water into Wine at *Cana* in *Galilee*, it was a Miracle perceivable by their Sight and Tafte ; had it ftill tafted and looked like Water, he and his Mother, and the Servants that filled the Water-pots, and bare it afterwards to the Governor of the Feaft, might have told the Governor, the Bridegroom, and the Gueft, that it was Wine over and over again till they had been weary, before they would have been able to perfuade them to believe it ; but the feeing and tafting that it was Wine, convinced them of the

(u) John vi. 14.

G 4

Mi-

Miracle.   Nor is it to be omitted (becaufe of
an Argument of the *Romanifts* that I fhall take
Notice of, and anfwer hereafter) that there is
particular Notice taken in this Place, that *(x)*
his Difciples believed on him when they faw this Mi-
racle, which manifefted forth his Glory ; in as much as
it took away all Doubt, and left no Room for any
Difbelief ; which muft have remained, maugre all
the moft pofitive Affertions that could have been
to the contrary, if the Species (or Accidents) of
Water (as the Papifts fay of the Bread and Wine)
had ftill remained ; becaufe nothing could have
been a fufficient Inducement to them to believe
or give Affent to any Thing without the Evidence of their Senfes, that being the very Means
that God has afforded all Mankind to judge of
any Thing by : And therefore fince God has
given us no other Faculties to judge of Miracles
by, but our Reafon and Senfes, all Miracles
muft be judged of by thofe Means ! Nor is there
in all the Scriptures of the Old or New Teftament, or in any human Author, that I have ever
heard or read of (till the Dream of Tranfubftantiation fprung up) any one Inftance of a Miracle
pretended to be wrought, but what was fubmitted to the Judgment of the People's Senfes.

Againft this Argument I never heard of any
Anfwer that could be offered, but that exceeding
weak one, which the *Romanifts* make ufe of on
this Occafion, *viz.* That Miracles wrought for
the Converfion of Unbelievers ought indeed to
be the Objects of our Senfes, but the Miracle of

(x) John ii. 11.

Tranfub-

Tranfubftantiation is not wrought on that Account, but for the Satisfaction of thofe that believe already; and for thefe latter it is fufficient,
that Chrift has faid, It is his Body, &c. fince
they know the Danger of not believing him more
than their Senfes. This is, I own, a very fhort
Way of folving a Difficulty, by cutting the Knot
they cannot untie! However, it is well they are
forced to grant, that Miracles ought to be the
Object of our Senfes, when wrought for the Converfion of Unbelievers; becaufe I fancy they will
find it a hard Tafk to give a good Reafon, why
the fame Method ought not to be taken, when
any Miracle is wrought for the Satisfaction, or
Confirmation of the Faith of Believers, as is
ufed for the Converfion of Unbelievers. For
their faying that it is enough, or that it is fufficient, that Chrift hath faid fo, or fo, will by
no means do; fince that is downright begging
the Queftion; it being utterly denied by us, who
are Believers as well as they, that Chrift faid thofe
Words in the Senfe wherein they interpret them,
which is the Thing to be proved, or elfe it fignifies nothing. Befides, this is contrary to what
we find in Scripture; for the Scriptures, both of
the Old and New Teftament, have, in an innumerable Number of Places, fhewn us, that Miracles have been very frequently wrought for the
Satisfaction of Believers; for by the Word *Be-*
lievers muft be underftood fuch Perfons as are
within the Pale of God's Church. The People
of *Ifrael* that were in *Egypt*, were the Defcen-
dants of *Abraham*, *Ifaac*, and *Jacob*, and Wor-
fhippers of God, according to the patriarchical
Church.

Church, which was then the Church of God, as we may fee by God's calling them (y) his People; and by their worfhipping him: And when they were come to Mount *Sinai*, and that the Law had been given them there, they were more peculiarly the Church of God; and efpecially the Tribe of *Levi*, who confecrated themfelves by flaying many of the Idolaters amongft the reft of the People, at the Command of *Mofes*; and therefore muft be allowed to be within the Pale of God's Church, and confequently Believers; and yet in the Sight of this People were all the Miracles of *Mofes* wrought, after their coming out of *Egypt*; for as to thofe which were wrought before *Pharaoh* and his Servants, perhaps it may be faid, they were wrought before Infidels, if not for their Converfion, yet at leaft for their Punifhment: I fay, the Miracles wrought by *Mofes* after the coming of the Children of *Ifrael* out of *Egypt*, were all of them the Objects of the Peoples Senfes; as the paffing of the *Red Sea*, the flowing of the Water out of the Rock, the Manna from Heaven, and the raining of Quails, were all of them Miracles wrought exprefsly to fatisfy that People, that the Lord their God was able to provide for them in all Manner of Places, how wild and barren foever the Country where they were might be. (z) The Rod that budded; the ftanding Miracle of the Anfwer by Urim, put into the Breaft-plate that was worn

(y) Exod. iii. 7. iv. 31. (z) Numb. xvii. 8. xxvii. 21. xxiii. 9, 11, 12. 1 Sam. xxviii. 6. xxx. 7, 8. Exod. xxv. 22. Numb. vii. 89.

upon

upon the Ephod by the High Prieft; the audible Voice from above the Cherubims on the Mercy-feat; and the Water of Jealoufy; were all Miracles to be performed before Believers, for their Satisfaction, and for the Confirmation of their Faith, &c. Not to infift upon thofe that were wrought for the Punifhment of wicked Believers, (a) as the Fire from Heaven that confumed *Korah* and his Company, and the Earthquake and Plague that enfued. But above all, the Miracles that were wrought for the Satisfaction of *Mofes* himfelf, were certainly of this Sort, *viz.* (b) His Rod that was turned into a Serpent; and the Leprofy of his own Hand; and the Cure of it again. Such likewife were thofe Miracles that were wrought by our Lord upon *Lazarus*, (c) when he raifed him from the Dead for the Satisfaction and Confirmation of the Faith of his Sifters, who had profeffed to believe him to be the Son of God; as well as of the Faith of the very Difciples themfelves; for whofe Sake he tells them, He was glad he was not there, that they might believe; might be ftill further fatisfied in their Belief, by feeing him raife up *Lazarus* from the Dead. There are many more that might be quoted, but I fhall inftance only in that of his Refurrection; for when he was defirous of fatisfying his Difciples beyond Contradiction or Doubt of the Truth of his Refurrection, he appeals to their Senfes, and bids

(a) Numb. xvi. 32, 35, 46.   (b) Exod. iv. 3, 4, 6, 7.   (c) John xi. 43, 44. 27. 15.

them

them (d) handle him, and see and behold his
Hands and his Feet, that it was he himself; and
as a further Confirmation, he performed before
them some of the Functions of Life, for he eat
of such Things as they gave him: He does not
tell them, as the Papists now do, that it is
enough, or it is sufficient, that I tell you, I am
risen from the Dead in the very same Body
wherein I suffered; or forewarn them of the
Danger of not believing him more than their
Senses; but on the contrary, (e) bids *Thomas* put
his Hand into his Side, and his Finger into the
Print of the Nails, that so he and the rest might
have the demonstrative Proof of Seeing and Feeling, for the Ground and Confirmation of their
Faith. Such were also those Miracles of Healing that were wrought by the Apostles, on such
Persons as were, doubtless, Believers before the
Miracles were wrought on them; as in the Instance of (f) *Tabitha* or *Dorcas*, who is expressly
said to be a Disciple, whom *Peter* raised from the
Dead; and it is highly credible that *Eneas*, who
was sick at *Lydda*, and was healed by the same
Apostle, was one of those Saints who are said to
dwell there; as also that *Eutichus*, who was
raised to Life again by St. *Paul*, was a Disciple,
for he was hearing St. *Paul* preach; but if not,
yet we cannot but believe, that he was raised to
Life again, for the Satisfaction and Confirmation
of the Faith of those other Disciples, who were
assembled there to break Bread, *i. e.* to receive

(d) Luke xxiv. 39, 40, 42, 43.   (e) John xx. 27.
(f) Acts ix. 36, 32, 33, 34. xx. 12.

the holy Sacrament (which is the Subject Matter of the prefent Difpute) and who were therefore certainly Believers; and fo of many others. So far is it from being true, that what Miracles are wrought for the Satisfaction and Confirmation of the Faith of Believers, are not neceffarily to be the Object of their Senfes, that not one can be inftanced in that was not made apparent to, and, fubmitted to the Judgment of fome one or more of them.

The all-merciful Goodnefs of God is, in my Opinion, a fure Pledge to us, that, if it had been neceffary to worfhip the Bread and Wine (which the Papifts call the natural Body and Blood of Chrift) in the Sacrament, we fhould not have been left under any Uncertainties in fo momentous an Affair, but the Scriptures would plainly have declared to us, that it was our Duty to do it, by commanding us fo to do in exprefs Terms, or by calling them Chrift or God; but the Scriptures having faid no more than what I have taken taken Notice of, I think it is a manifeft Sign, that God never intended we fhould pay divine Worfhip to them. This Silence of the Scriptures, which were written (g) by the Infpiration of God, purpofely to make us *wife unto Salvation, and thoroughly furnifhed unto all good Works,* and which confequently contain in them the Knowledge of all Doctrines and Inftructions neceffary to be believed and practifed by thofe who fhall be Heirs of Salvation; is the more to be infifted on, either if the Good-

(g) 2 Tim. iii. 15, 16, 17.

ness of God, as I said before, which leads
him to inform his Creatures of all necessary
Truths, be duely considered ; or if we compare
therewith the copious Declarations which the
holy Scriptures have made concerning the Divinity of our blessed Saviour, which could not be
so intirely hid under the Veil of human Shape,
as, upon the Supposition of Transubstantiation,
it must certainly be allowed to be under that of
Bread and Wine ; and yet, because by his taking
(h) *upon him the Form of a Servant* ; and his being
made in the Likeness ; *and found in the Fashion of
a Man* ; and by his humbling himself, and be-
coming obedient to the Death of the Cross ; his
Godhead might be so clouded, as to stand in
need of express Declarations to discover it to us ;
God has not contented himself to ascribe to our
Saviour, in very many Places of Scripture, the
Divine Attributes and Properties of the Godhead ; but hath expressly told us, by our Lord's
own Mouth, That (i) we ought to *honour the
Son even as we honour the Father* ; (of whom *John*
also bare Record, that he was *the Son of God*)
and that the Works which he did, and the Con-
currence of the Scriptures, testified of him ; and
hath assured us by St. *Paul*, in his Epistle to the
Philippians, That (k) God hath *given him a
Name, which is above every Name, that at the
Name of Jesus every Knee should bow, and that
every Tongue should confess, that Jesus Christ is
Lord to the Glory of God the Father :* Meaning

(h) Phil. ii. 7, 8.   (i) John v. 23. i. 34. v. 36,
39.   (k) Phil. ii. 9, 10, 11.

thereby,

thereby, that it is to the Glory even of God the
Father, that we fhould confefs that Jefus Chrift
is the Lord or God. And in his Epiftle to the
Hebrews, he tells us, That (l) when God brought
this *firſt-begotten into the World*, he commanded
all his holy Angels to worſhip him. This the
Holy Ghoſt hath thought neceſſary thus plainly
to declare to us concerning the Divinity of our
bleſſed Saviour Jefus Chriſt ; although, as I ſaid
before, it could not be ſo ſtrange or unlikely a
Thing to the *Jews*, with whom he converſed,
or to us, to whom his Hiſtory, Doctrines and
Precepts are tranſmitted, that he ſhould take our
human Nature upon him, as that he ſhould veil
his Godhead under the Shape or Appearance of
the inanimate Creatures of Bread and Wine ;
ſeeing he had very frequently (m) manifeſted
himſelf in the Likeneſs of Man to the Patriarchs
of old. Our Saviour Jefus Chriſt, who was (n)
Emanuel, or *God with us*, or *God manifeſt in the
Fleſh*, gave many Proofs of his Divinity. He is
frequently ſaid to know the Thoughts of Man ;
which is an Attribute of the Godhead ; the
Knowledge of the Heart and of the Thoughts
being Attributes which *David* and St. *Peter* aſcribe
particularly to God. Our Saviour alſo ſuffered
himſelf to be worſhipped, not only when he was
an Infant (when perhaps it may be objected, that

(l) Heb. i. 6.   (m) Gen. xviii. 10, 17, 20.
xxxii. 24, 30. Joſhua v. 13, 14, 15.   (n) Matt.
i. 23. 1 Tim. iii. 16. Matt. ix. 4. Mark ii. 8.
John ii. 25. Pſalm xxvi. 2. cxxxix. 2. Acts ii. 24.
xv. 8.

he

he could not prevent it) by the (o) wife Men, by the proper Sacrifice of Incenfe and other Offerings; but likewife during his publick Miniftry; by the (p) Leper whom he cleanfed; by *Jairus*, the Ruler of the Synagogue; by the Man that was born blind, whofe Eyes he opened; and many others. If therefore God has thought it neceffary fo particularly to tranfmit to us, that our Saviour was to be adored, and that too even by the (q) Angels themfelves; and to make known to us, that he was *the Brightnefs of his Glory, and the exprefs Image of his Perfon*; that he was his Son, *the only-begotten of the Father*; and fometimes by a Voice from Heaven, that he was his *beloved Son:* How much greater Reafon have we to expect, that fome particular Declaration fhould have been made in Scripture, that the Bread and Wine, if tranfubftantiated into Chrift Jefus, was to be the Object of our Adoration? The Truth of which, nothing lefs than a divine, exprefs and plain Declaration can be fufficient to convince us of.

My great Love for you, and the tender Regard I have for the Perfon you have married, in as much as fhe is your Wife, whofe Converfion I therefore think it my Duty to endeavour, and fhould be glad to be any way inftrumental in, has made me take the Pains to confider this Controverfy about Idolatry in the ftricteft and fulleft Manner I was able; becaufe it is more than pro-

(o) Matt. ii. 11.   (p) Matt. viii. 3. Luke viii. 41. John ix. 38.   (q) Heb. i. 6. 3. John i. 14. Matt. iii. 17. xvii. 5.

bable

bable that every *Romanist*, who believes and prac-
tises according to what is declared to be the Doctrine and Practice of the Church of *Rome*, must
be guilty of Idolatry ; not only in what they
teach concerning Angels, Saints, &c. but more
especially in what they enjoin relating to the
Adoration of the Host ; nay, it is certain and
inevitable almost to a Demonstration.   For the
Council of *Trent*, and the Missal and Rituals of
that Church (which are the Rules by which the
Papists are to guide themselves, as to Doctrine,
Discipline and Worship) having positively required and enjoined all Christians to worship the
holy Sacrament, and declared that they ought
so to do, (r) with the same Veneration that is
due to the true God ; and having declared what
Requisites were necessary (s) to the consecrating
the Host with due Effect ; if then those Requisites, or any of them, be wanting ; and the Host
be not, by reason of such Defect, transubstantiated into Christ, every such *Romanist* so adoring
the Host, must be guilty of Idolatry.   For sup-
posing (though not granting) that the Host, or
the Bread, &c. when duely consecrated, is transubstantiated or converted into the Body of our
Lord ; yet, according to the Rules and Doctrines
of that Church, unless it be duely consecrated
with Effect, it is not so much as pretended to be
transubstantiated or converted into the Body, &c.
of our Lord ; but the Means whereby (according
to the Rules laid down in that Church) it may

(r) Counc. Trent, sect. 13. ch. 5.   (s) Rom.
Miss. of Defects, p. 35.

H

happen,

happen, that the Bread, *&c.* is not duely confecrated, are very many ; therefore it is almoſt inevitable but that, upon the Foot of their own Doctrine, every *Romaniſt* ſo believing or adoring muſt be guilty of Idolatry. For it is their ſettled Determination, that there can be no Tranſubſtantiation in the Sacrament, unleſs the Conſecration be without Defect ; but the Conſecration, according to the Requiſites laid down in the *Roman* Miſſal, may be defective any of theſe ſeveral Ways : (s) If the Perſon conſecrating happen to diminiſh or alter any of the Words of Conſecration, ſo that the Senſe be varied, or that any one Word belonging to the Form be omitted, then the Tranſubſtantion is not effected ; if by Mixture with any other Grain (which no Prieſt, or Communicant, or any other Perſon, but the Miller that grinds, or he that ſells the Flour, or he that bakes the Wafer or Bread, can certainly know) it be not Wheaten Bread ; or if the Bread or Wine be any way ſpoiled, the Conſecration is not done with Effect ; (t) or it may happen, in caſe the Prieſt that performs the Office have no Intention to conſecrate the Bread and Wine ; or if he be an Atheiſt, or a *Jew* (of which laſt Sort it is frequently found that there are many in *Spain* and *Portugal*) ; or if he be not a Prieſt, *i. e.* was not rightly baptized or ordained, (u) as to the Matter, or Form, or the Intention of him that baptized or ordained him ; or if that Baptiſm or Ordination was done by one

(s) Rom. Miſſ. of Defects, p. 35.   (t) Ibid.
p. 34.   (u) Ibid. p. 36,

that

that was no Prieſt himſelf; or if the Conſecration of the Elements in the Sacrament be not
performed (x) with a low Voice (and in caſe it
be ſo performed, it is impoſſible for a Lay-Com-
municant to know whether the Senſe be not varied or altered, or whether there be no Words
left out); or if the ſame be performed in the
vulgar Tongue (and if it be not, no Perſon that
is ignorant of the *Latin,* as moſt Women, and
many Men are, can know whether it be or be
not done as it ought) then the Conſecration is
not rightly performed, nor the Tranſubſtantiation
effected. For if any of theſe Defects happen *(y),*
the Bread and Wine is held, by that Church itſelf, not to be tranſubſtantiated; and conſequently
the Object worſhipped is ſtill Bread and Wine,
whereby the Adoration is paid, even according to their own Doctrine, to a Creature, which
is Idolatry. So that were there nothing elſe to
be ſaid againſt the Belief of this Article of Faith
in the *Roman* Church, yet theſe Difficulties and
Requiſites conſidered, I think I may fairly pronounce, that All Papiſts believing as that Church
directs, and practiſing the Worſhip She commands, muſt, for any Thing they can poſſibly
know to the contrary, be guilty of Idolatry!
Which ought to ſtrike a ſerious and conſidering
Papiſt with the greateſt Horror imaginable!

To this I know it is ſometimes alledged by
the Defenders of that Church (eſpecially when
they are endeavouring to convert a Proteſtant,

(x) Counc. Trent, ſect. 22. ch. 9.　　(y) Rom.
Miſſ. p. 34, 35.

or confirm a Papift whom they think wavering) that it is impoffible to imagine, that the wilful Default of fuch as are to prepare the Bread and Wine; or any Defect in the Elements; or the Wickednefs of the Prieft who is to perform the Confecration (if he could be guilty of fo great a Villainy, as the not intending duely to confe-crate the Elements) fhould hinder the Tranfub-ftantiation, and thereby make an innocent Per-fon that receives the fame, guilty of the Sin of Idolatry. They may alledge this as long as they pleafe, but what I afferted is neverthelefs the natural Confequence of the Tenets, which they do pofitively hold and teach; for it is plainly the Doctrine of the Church of *Rome*, that in cafe there happens any of the afore-mentioned De-fects, and particularly *if the Intention of the Prieft be wanting*, it is (z) fufficient to hinder the Tran-fubftantiation, which, unlefs it be effected, they do not themfelves pretend, but that the Elements remain Bread and Wine, as before the Words of Confecration were pronounced; and then the Bread and Wine being adored by the Commu-nicant, who knows nothing of the Defect, the Adorer idolizes a Creature, which is Idolatry; becaufe all Adoration paid to any Being, but God, is Idolatry. But how ftrange and hard foever this Charge upon the Papifts, from the Defects of the Elements, or the Wickednefs of the Priefts, may feem to be, it is not only what they pofitively declare in this Cafe, which is fuf-ficient to juftify the Charge; but it is agreeable

(z) Rom. Miff. p. 34.

to the like abfurd and impious Doctrine of theirs in the Sacrament of Baptifm, and their additional Sacraments of Penance and Abfolution ; for the Council of *Trent* anathematizes in fo many (a) Words, all fuch as hold that the Intention of the Prieft is not neceffary to the due Celebration of their Sacraments, or that do not believe, (b) that where the due Matter, or Form, with Intention is wanting, the Confecration is not performed. And further declare, (c) that no one ought to flatter himfelf, that he can be faved by his own Faith, and abfolved before God, though he have true Contrition and Repentance, unlefs the Prieft ferioufly and truly intended to abfolve him : From whence may be drawn this moft uncomfortable Inference to the Penitent (I fpeak with regard to fuch as believe the Priëfts have Power to abfolve them) that the Prieft may gravely pronounce the Words of Abfolution over him, and yet that he may be eternally damned, though he is never fo truly penitent and contrite for his Sins, becaufe the Prieft is wicked enough, not to *intend* to abfolve him.   And here I muft obferve, that it can be no Breach of Charity in us to fuppofe fome of the Priefts wicked enough to ufe the Forms appointed at the Confecration or Celebration of their Sacraments, without Intention to confecrate, *&c.* fince the Church of *Rome* herfelf has thought it poffible, by declaring, in fo many Places as fhe does, that where it is

(a) Counc. Trent, fect. 7. ch. 1.   (b) Rom. Miff. p. 34.   (c) Counc. Trent, fect. 7. ch. 6.

H 3   wanting,

wanting, such Sacrament is not duely performed, that is, though it be indeed performed outwardly, yet it will be without Effect; for there will be in that Case no Transubstantiation in the Sacrament of the Lord's Supper, nor any Forgiveness from those of Baptism, Penance, or Absolution!

I am now to answer that Part of your Letter of the 24th of *August* 1725, which has Relation to your Marriage. You will see by my former Letter, as well as by those I have written you this Year, that I have no other Dissatisfaction to your Marriage, but that your Wife is of the *Romish* Church; had it not been for that, I should on the contrary have been highly pleased with it, in as much as I hear she is a Woman of Virtue and Discretion; and though she is a Papist, yet should she be convinced of the Errors of Popery, and forsake them, I should then be very well pleased with, and approve of your Choice; but till then, I cannot help being extreamly uneasy at so great an Unhappiness. You will easily imagine from hence, that I am very glad to find by the Postscript to that Letter, that you are not without Hopes of bringing her over to your Religion (God grant it may be so); for which you give the following Reasons; *viz.* " That she does not allow of the worshipping " of Images, or the praying to Saints; that she " thinks reading the Scriptures necessary; that she " is not of Opinion, that Confession is absolutely " necessary; and that she differs from us in scarce " any Thing, but in the real Presence, Purga- " tory, and the Difference of Sins; and then " you beg my Prayers for her thorough Conver- " sion."

" fion." I affure you, my Dear, I offer up my Prayers to God for her Converfion very ferioufly, and I hope God will in his infinite Mercy hear and grant them; which I make no doubt but you will be fully fatisfied of, when you fee by this Letter, that I have not fpared my Pains, but have endeavoured to convince her of the Sins and Errors practifed and allowed of, in the Church of *Rome*, by fuch Arguments, as I hope may be effectual with a Woman of Candour and Senfe. Perhaps fhe and you may both think I might have fhortened my own Trouble in writing, and yours in reading, fo long an Epiftle, by not touching at all on the Subject of Images and Saints; fince you fay fhe does not allow of the worfhipping of the one, or the praying to the other: But there being two Objects of Idolatry, *viz.* the Praying to Angels, and the Adoration of the Hoft, which are not mentioned in your Letter amongft thofe which fhe difallows, though perhaps they were only omitted, and fhe may, notwithftanding that Omiffion, not hold with her Church therein; yet as that does not appear to me, and that there is fo clofe a Connection between the feveral Branches of Idolatry, as taught and practifed in that Church, I was willing to confider that Subject in all its Parts. And the rather, becaufe if fhe is once fatisfied, that that Church is idolatrous in any one Branch of their Belief or Practice, I hope fhe will think herfelf bound in Confcience to forfake that Religion, and to hold no Communion with a Church that enjoins its Votaries to live in the Commiffion of the moft flagrant of all Sins; and that (notwithftanding

fhe

she should think the rest of their Doctrines to be true and well-grounded, which I hope to shew her they are not, yet that) she ought to follow the Advice and Command of St. *Paul*, in his second Epistle to the *Corinthians*, when he exhorts them (d) to fly from the Society and Pollution of Idolaters; seeing, as he adds, *the Temple of God*, which Temple he tells them they were, can have no Agreement with Idols, and therefore commands them (e) to come out from amongst, and to be separate from them; and then assures them, as an Encouragement for their so doing, that God would be their Father, and they should be his Children : From whence this Inference is very natural; that, as God would be their Father, and they should be his Children, if they did forsake Communion with Idolaters; so, by Parity of Reason, that he will not be their Father, nor should they be his Children, if they did not.

I shall now consider the rest of the Articles you mention, either as allowed or disallowed of by her; which I shall do very briefly, because, as I said before, having fully shewn the Sinfulness of the Idolatry practised in the Church of *Rome*, I have thereby shewn, not only how dangerous it is to continue therein, but likewise how necessary it is to leave it; that having been the crying Sin that God has always found fault with at all Times, and in all Nations; as may be seen throughout the whole Scripture of the Old Testament. That Sin was so provoking in his

(d) 2 Cor. vi. 16.   (e) Ibid. ver. 17, 18.

Sight,

Sight, that it was always the Cause of his with-drawing his Protection from the Children of *Is-rael*, and of his delivering them up to their Ene-mies; as you may read in almost every Chapter of the Books of the Prophets. And in the New Testament, St. *John* closes his general Epistle with bidding them, to whom he wrote, (f) to keep themselves *from Idols*; as if it were placed last, and seemingly without any Relation to the Context, on purpose that they should take the greater Care to observe that particular Precept. St. *Paul* likewise cautions the *Corinthians* not to be (g) *Idolaters*, left they should be overthrown or destroyed as the *Israelites* were; the Example of whose Punishments ought to teach them to avoid falling into the like Sin, because those Things were written for their Admonition: And then bids them *flee from Idolatry*; for they could not be Partakers of the Cup or Table of the Lord, and the Cup or Table of Devils; there being so great a Contrariety between the Service of God and the Service of Idols, which is the Ser-vice of Devils, that they could not be Partakers of both. And therefore whensoever Idolatry is enjoined or practised in any Church, it is a suf-ficient Reason of itself, without any other, to lay an Obligation upon its Members to with-draw from its Communion: So that though the Falseness of the other Points in question between us, may aggravate the Sinfulness of continuing in Communion with the Church of *Rome,* yet

(f) 1 John v. 21. (g) 1 Cor. x. 7. 5. 11, 14, 19, 20, 21.

the

the Truth of such Points (suppoſing, but not granting, that were the Caſe) would not be ſufficient to juſtify Continuance with her, or to render her Communion innocent.

I obſerve you ſay, ſhe holds it neceſſary to read the Scriptures; to confirm her in which Perſuaſion, I recommend to her the reading of Archbiſhop *Tillotſon's Rule of Faith*: Wherein ſhe will find how much a more excellent Way the Scriptures muſt needs be, of conveying to us the Knowledge of God's Will, than that much-cried-up one amongſt the Papiſts, of oral Tradition. The Happineſs of having the Scriptures to guide us is, by St. *Peter*, preferred even before the Hearing of a Voice from Heaven : For, after he had mentioned, that (b) *it was from his own Experience, that he made known to them* (to whom he wrote his Epiſtle) *the Power and Coming of our Lord Jeſus Chriſt, he being an Eye and-Ear-witneſs of his Transfiguration,* when he heard a Voice from Heaven, declaring him to be the *Well-beloved Son of God,* he ſays, (i) *There was yet a more ſure Word of Prophecy,* which he praiſes them for taking heed to, *ſince no Prophecy of the Scripture was of any private Interpretation, but holy Men ſpoke as they were moved by the Holy Ghoſt.* Agreeably to what St. *Paul* tells *Timothy,* when he commends him (k) *for having known the holy Scriptures from his Childhood;* that *all Scriptures were written by the Inſpiration of God, and were proper for Doctrine, for Reproof, for Correction,*

(b) 2 Pet. i. 16, 17.   (i) Ibid. ver. 19, 20, 21.
(k) 2 Tim. iii. 15, 16, 17.

for

for Instruction in Righteousness, that the Man of God (or all Christians) *might be perfect, and thoroughly furnished unto all good Works.* (i) *For they were written for our Admonition, and for our Learning, and are able to make us wise unto Salvation* ; the reading whereof is also recommended by our Saviour, when he tells the *Jews*, that (k) *they should search the Scriptures, for they are they which testify of him.* The royal Prophet, amongst other Descriptions of a Man that might be termed *blessed*, says, (l) *That his Delight is in the Law of the Lord, and in his Law will he meditate*, or exercise himself, *Day and Night* ; and (m) *That his own Practice was to meditate on God's Precepts* ; and (n) *That God's Word was a Lamp unto his Feet, and a Light unto his Paths.* ——That your Wife may then meditate on God's Word with the greater Advantage to her Soul, I would advise her to learn the Collect for the Second *Sunday* in *Advent*, and to repeat it to herself whenever she is going to hear or read any Portions of the holy Scriptures : It is my own Practice ; and I verily believe I may say, I have reaped Benefit from my constantly using that Prayer before my reading the Scripture ; which I likewise recommend to your own Practice. I would likewise advise you both, that, when you read of any Promises of Pardon to repenting Sinners, you would put up a short Ejaculation to God, that he would in like Manner grant you Forgiveness thro' the Merits of Christ,

(i) 1 Cor. x. 11. Rom. xv. 4. 1 Tim. iii. 15. (k) John v. 39. (l) Psalm i. 2. (m) Psalm cxix. 15. (n) Ibid. ver. 105.

upon

upon your true Repentance; any Threatenings against obstinate Offenders, that he would be pleased to turn your Hearts, give you his restraining Grace, prevent your Impenitence, and avert his Judgments from you, for the Sake of his well-beloved Son; when you meet with any plain Passages in Scripture for Instruction in Righteousness, then praise God for his Mercy in affording Sinners so clearly the Knowledge of what he would them believe and practise; any Passages in holy Writ which are too obscure and hard for you to comprehend, pray, that God would be pleased, in his good Time, to enlighten your Understanding to know his Will, or at least not to impute to you the Want of such Knowledge; and, like the Man that came to our Saviour to have his Son healed, profess, that (m) *though you believe*, yet you do, with the greatest Sincerity, desire *that he would help your Unbelief* (n). When you have thus piously offered up the Sacrifice of your Hearts to God, you may assure yourselves, that he will, of his infinite Goodness, afford you all the Light and Grace which he thinks necessary for you; and, that what he does not afford you, he will not require of you; for Christ has told us, (o) *That if any Man is desirous to do the Will of God, he shall know of the Doctrine whether it be of God*; but if we wilfully shut our Eyes against, or will not make use of, the Means of Grace that are afforded us, he is no Ways bound irresistably to open them for us. I think these Rules for reading the Scriptures con-

(m) Mark ix. 24.　　　(n) By which is meant not absolute Infidelity, but only Imperfection in Belief.

(o) John vii. 17.

stantly,

ftantly, or at leaft frequently practifed with humble and fincere Attention, muft, by God's Grace, have a good Effect upon your Lives and Converfations, and make you *(n) blamelefs and harmlefs, the Children of God, without Rebuke, in the Midft of a crooked and perverfe Generation ;* and *(o) that others, feeing your good Works, will glorify your Father which is in Heaven.* This is what I think fufficient to fay, in order to encourage her in her Refolution, and to fhew the Advantages and Neceffity of being thoroughly acquainted with the holy Scriptures.

The next Thing you mention is, That fhe is not of Opinion, that Confeffion is abfolutely neceffary. I fuppofe you mean here, Confeffion to a Prieft ; for Confeffion to God is abfolutely neceffary, but that to a Prieft is not fo ; nor do I believe it would be thought fo, even in their Church, were it not very ftrenuoufly inculcated into the Minds of the Laity by the Priefts, becaufe they can by Means thereof maintain their too great Authority the better. You will have taken Notice, that I have already, in this Letter *(p)*, juft mentioned how uncomfortable that Doctrine muft needs be which teaches, That let a Penitent in the Church of *Rome* be never fo ferious in his Repentance, and truly contrite for his Sins, yet that his Salvation intirely depends upon the Pleafure of the Prieft, who may, it is true, pronounce the Words of Abfolution to him, but without intending to abfolve him ;

(n) Philip. ii. 15.   (o) Matt. v. 16.   (p) See before, page 101.

without

without which Intention the Abſolution is held
by that Church to be invalid (q); and therefore
for any Efficacy from that Abſolution the Penitent may be damned; and, if another Part of
their Doctrine be true, he not only may, but
muſt be, damned, when the Prieſt does not intend to abſolve him; becauſe the Council of
Trent (r) hold the adminiſtering the Sacrament
of Penance neceſſary to Salvation in all that fall,
or ſin after Baptiſm; and, as no Sacrament can
be valid without the Intention of the Prieſt (s),
therefore, where Penance and Abſolution are
impoſed and given without Intention, they can
be of no Efficacy, and conſequently the Perſon
depending thereon, if that Doctrine be true, muſt
be damned. I repeat this only with Deſign to
ſhew a conſidering Papiſt, the Abſurdity and Im-
piety of the *Romiſh* Doctrine of Confeſſion to a
Prieſt, whoſe Intention to abſolve, the Penitent
(which is what he aims at by his confeſſing to
him) is held neceſſary in that Church, to effect
his Pardon in the next World; for, with reſpect
to the Thing itſelf, or to us Proteſtants, it is of
no Moment at all whether the Prieſt does, or
does not, intend his Abſolution ſhould be effica-
tious, becauſe we do not depend either upon his
Intention, or Abſolution, but upon God only
for our Pardon; believing the Prieſts to have no
other Power of Abſolution, than what is merely
declaratory; that is, to declare and pronounce,
That God will pardon and abſolve thoſe who do truly

(q) Council of Trent, ſect. 7. ch. 6.   (r) Ibid.
ſect. 14. ch. 2.   (s) Ibid. ſect. 7. ch. 1.

and

and sincerely repent of their Sins, and unfeignedly believe the Gospel (t); which is all the Power we believe them to have in this Matter. Besides, the Doctrine of Confession, as practised in the Church of *Rome*, has a Tendency to make People more wicked than they would be, if they had a true Notion of confessing to God only : For, if I am not mistaken in the Practice amongst the *Romanists*, the Manner of their Confession, the Easiness of procuring the outward Absolution of the Priest (for whether his inward Intention go with it, or not, cannot be known by the Person confessing) and the Satisfaction they think they make for their Sins, by suffering the Penances imposed upon them as a commutative Satisfaction, are much more like to embolden them to continue in the Commission of their Sins and Impieties, than effectually to deter them from repeating the same, or from committing the like again : For it is certain, that the Love of Sin, in the Generality of Mankind, is so great, that so long as they believe themselves assured of Pardon upon confessing their Sins to a Priest, and receiving his Absolution, which they (not knowing his inward Thoughts) believe to be efficacious to their Salvation, there is no Penance can be thought of but they would willingly undergo it, if they could thereby wipe off the old Score, that so they might begin again ; and in this Manner continue alternately confessing, and sinning afresh : Whereas our Doctrine, that Confession must be made to God only, and

(t) Form of Absolution in the Morning and Evening Service in our Liturgy.

that

that with the greateſt Sorrow, and the trueſt Contrition, for our Sins ; with the moſt ardent Deſires, that he would be pleaſed, for the Sake of Chriſt Jeſus our Lord, to forgive us the Guilt and Puniſhment of thoſe Sins which we thus ſeriouſly repent of, and unfeignedly reſolve to forſake, muſt have a very different Effect. This Manner of confeſſing ourſelves to God, which keeps us ſtill penitent before that awful Majeſty who we are ſenſible knows our Hearts, and whether our Repentance is truly ſincere or not, and whom we know we cannot deceive ; I ſay, this Doctrine and Practice muſt be much more productive of a holy Life, and of that Abhorrence which we ought to have for Sin ; and be much more likely to make us careful to avoid the Commiſſion of what requires ſo ſtrict and ſolemn an Humiliation and Repentance, than that of confeſſing our Sins to a Prieſt, at ſuch and ſuch ſet Times, which, after we are a little uſed to, like plunging into the Water, ceaſes to be any Pain or Uneaſineſs, and becomes familiar to us, and is looked upon, I am verily perſuaded, by moſt Perſons, to be Matter of mere Form. Further, the Notion of Abſolution is impertinent and nonſenſical, if it be meant in any other Senſe than that of being declaratory or optative ; *declaratory*, in pronouncing that *Almighty God, of his great Mercy, hath promiſed Forgiveneſs of Sins to all them that with hearty Repentance, and true Faith, turn unto him* (u) ; optative, in wiſhing

(u) The Form of Confeſſion and Abſolution in the Communion Service of the Engliſh Liturgy.

that *he would have Mercy upon all thofe who acknowledge and bewail their manifold Sins and Wickednefs,* from time to time moft grievoufly committed, by *Thought,* *Word,* or *Deed,* againft his
divine Majefty; and praying, *That he would pardon and deliver thofe who do earneftly repent, and
are heartily forry for their Mifdoings,* and *whofe
Sins are grievous, and an intolerable Burden, unto
them:* For, though there is another Form of Abfolution ufed by fome of our Minifters, when
the fick Perfon heartily defires it (x), that carries with it feemingly a more pofitive Senfe (the
literal Wording whereof I cannot fo perfectly juftify) yet the Meaning of it is ftill the fame with
the Two other Forms already mentioned; as we
muft certainly conclude from hence, That, were
it intended to be underftood as abfolutely efficacious to the Salvation of the Perfon to whom it
is fpoken (as the Words, without further Confideration, feem to imply) there would have been
no need of the Collect or Prayer that (does not
go before, but) immediately follows the pronouncing the Abfolution; in the ufing of which
Prayer, the Prieft, by faying, *Let us pray,* exhorts and invites not only the fick Perfon himfelf, but likewife all the other Communicants
that are there (if there be any other Perfons prefent, as there moft commonly is) to join with
him in praying to God; *who, according to the
Multitude of his Mercies, puts away the Sins of*

(x) Form of Abfolution in the Vifitation of the
Sick. *Englifh* Liturgy.

I

thofe

thofe who truly repent (y) ; that for as much as the Penitent puts his full Truft only in God's Mercy (not in the Abfolution he had received the Moment before from the Prieft) he (God) *would not impute unto him his former Sins, but ftrengthen him with the bleffed Spirit* ; and then concludes by praying, *That, when he is pleafed to take him hence, he would take him into his Favour* (it is not faid for the Sake, or by Virtue, of the Prieft's Abfolution, but) *through the Merits of his moft dearly beloved Son Chrift Jefus our Lord :* I fay, the Notion of Abfolution, in any other Senfe than this, is impertinent and nonfenfical : *Impertinent*, to *plague* Mankind with obliging them to believe, that the Abfolution of a Prieft is any otherwife neceffary than only, *in general*, by declaring, that God will forgive all thofe who bewail their own Sinfulnefs, and confefs themfelves unto God, with full Purpofe to amend their Lives ; and, *in particular*, by wifhing or praying (z), That the Perfons, who cannot, perhaps, quiet their own Confciences, by Reafon of the Heinoufnefs of their Sins (and therefore come to a Prieft for Counfel and Comfort) may be of the Number of thofe who receive the Benefit of Abfolution according to the Miniftry of God's Word, who hath promifed Pardon to all them that with hearty Repentance, and true Faith, turn unto him : *Nonfenfical*, to fuppofe that God would give away his own Power of pardoning a Sinner, and grant

(y) Colle&t next after the faid Abfolution.
(z) Exhortation to prepare for receiving the Communion. *Englifh* Common Prayer-Book.

fuch

such a supereminent Privilege to his Ministers, as (if I may be allowed to use the Expression) would make a Divorce between his Power and his Justice, or his Mercy ; for that must be the Case, if the Minister or Priest hath an absolute Option whether he will effectually grant a Sinner his Pardon in the next World, or not. Because, if the Absolution of a Priest, pronounced seriously, and with Intention really to save the Person confessing, be absolutely efficacious to procure him the Pardon of his Sins, by virtue of the Power which it is pretended was committed to the Priests for that Purpose by Christ (and if he hath not this Option, or that his Absolution be not absolutely, but only conditionally (if God sees fit) efficacious to the Salvation of the Sinner, such Popish Priest, and his Absolution, have really no greater Power or Virtue than what we allow to our Protestant Ministers, and their Absolution, which is to be declaratory or optative only ; and then the Pother and Rout they make about this Matter is of no Moment, but is vain and ridiculous ; but, if it hath that Privilege of absolutely pardoning) then the Sinner (whatever in the mean Time becomes of him in Purgatory, which shall be considered of hereafter) must sooner or later go to Heaven : So that though God sees the Heart of the Person absolved, and knows that he is an Hypocrite, and not truly penitent, yet he has it not in his Power to condemn him to Hell, or to disannul in the next World, the Pardon given him by the Priest in this : And, on the contrary, seeing Penance and Absolution are held necessary to Salvation, if the Priest re-

I 2   fuses

fufes to abfolve a Sinner, or (which is all one with them) does not do it with a ferious and full Intention that the Penance he impofes, or the Abfolution he pronounces, fhould be efficacious to the Sinner's Salvation ; though God fees his Heart, and knows that he is truly penitent, and that he intends to lead a new Life ; and is one of thofe, who not only (a) *confeffes with his Mouth the Lord Jefus, but believes in his Heart, that God hath raifed him from the Dead* ; as likewife, that (b) *he has recovered himfelf out of the Snare of the Devil, by Repentance, which God has vouchfafed him to the Acknowledgment of the Truth* ; yet the Mercy of God cannot be exercifed towards fuch a Sinner in the next World,, becaufe he is precluded therefrom, by reafon that the Prieft, upon his Confeffion, did not impofe his Penance, and give him Abfolution, with Intent that they fhould be efficacious to his Salvation.

As to her Belief of the real Prefence ; if fhe means thereby, as I am afraid fhe does, what the Church of *Rome* does by Tranfubftantiation, *viz.* The Change, or Tranfubftantiation, of the Bread and Wine into the natural Body and Blood of Chrift ; I hope I have faid enough already in the foregoing Part of this Letter, under the Head of Idolatry in adoring the Hoft, to convince her, both from Scripture and Reafon, that the Thing is not only impoffible, but that our Saviour never intended to have his Words underftood in that Senfe ; to which I fhall therefore refer her back, having there faid what I thought the Subject re-

(a) Rom. x. 9.   (b) 2 Tim. ii. 25, 26.

quired,

quired, that I might avoid the Neceffity of mentioning it over again in this Place. But if by
real Prefence fhe means, that (c) whenever, with
a true penitent Heart, and lively Faith, we receive the holy Sacrament, we fpiritually eat the
Flefh of Chrift, and drink his Blood ; and that
when we receive the Creatures of Bread and
Wine (d), according to the holy Inftitution of
Chrift, and in Remembrance of his Death and
Paffion, we become Partakers of his moft bleffed
Body and Blood, and that (e) by fo duly receive-
ing thofe holy Myfteries, we are fed with the
fpiritual Food of his moft precious Body and
Blood ; and do thereby become very or true
Members, incorporate in the myftical *Body* of
Chrift, which is the bleffed Company of all faithful People. If this Suftenance of the Soul, this
fpiritual Food, this fpiritual Prefence, and not
the corporeal Prefence, of Chrift's natural Flefh
and Blood, be what fhe means by real Prefence
(and a Spirit is as truly a Being, or real Effence,
as a Body is) it is the fame that we Proteftants
believe ; which I think it is impoffible for Words
to exprefs better than thofe do that our Church
hath made ufe of, in the Rubrick after the Office
for the Communion of the Sick, and in the Articles of our Church, concerning the Lord's Supper ; with both which Quotations I fhall clofe
this Head : (f) " That if a Man, by Reafon of

(c) Exhortation before the Communion. *Englifh*
Liturgy. (d) Prayer of Confecration. (e) Second Thankfgiving after receiving. (f) Rubrick
after the Office for the Communion of the Sick.
Englifh Liturgy.

I 3 " Ex-

" Extremity of Sickneſs, or other juſt Impedi-
" ment, do not receive the Sacrament of Chriſt's
" Body and Blood, the Curate ſhall inſtruct him,
" that if he do truly repent him of his Sins, and
" ſtedfaſtly believe that Jeſus Chriſt hath ſuffer-
" ed Death upon the Croſs for him, and ſhed
" his Blood for his Redemption, earneſtly re-
" membering the Benefits he hath (or reaps)
" thereby, and giving him Thanks therefore (or
" for the ſame) he doth eat and drink the Body
" and Blood of our Saviour profitably to his
" Soul's Health, although he doth not receive
" the Sacrament with his Mouth." (g) " To
" ſuch as right worthily, and with Faith, re-
" ceive the ſame, the Bread which we brake is
" a Partaking of the Body of Chriſt, and like-
" wiſe the Cup of Bleſſing is a Partaking of the
" Blood of Chriſt. The Body of Chriſt is
" given, taken, and eaten in the Supper, only
" after an heavenly and ſpiritual Manner. And
" the Means whereby the Body of Chriſt is re-
" ceived, and eaten in the Supper, is, Faith."
(h) " The Wicked, and ſuch as be void of a
" lively Faith, although they do carnally and
" viſibly preſs with their Teeth the Sacrament
" of the Body and Blood of Chriſt ; yet in no-
" wiſe are they Partakers of Chriſt, but rather
" do eat and drink the Sign or Sacrament of ſo
" great a Thing (i)." But, if Tranſubſtantiation
be true, they muſt not only receive the Sign or

(g) 28th Article of Religion.   (h) 29th Article
of Religion.   (i) This is what St. *Paul* calls *eating unworthily*, i. e. not diſcerning, *the Lord's Body*,
1 Cor. xi. 27, 29.

Sacrament

Sacrament (that is, the Myftery) of fo great a Thing, but the Thing itfelf, the very natural Body and Blood of Chrift.

As to her Belief of the Difference of Sins : Though I fhall plainly and pofitively affirm with the Scripture, that (h) *whofoever committeth Sin, tranfgreffeth the Law,* and that (i) *all Unrighteouf-nefs is Sin,* and, confequently, that all Unrigh-teoufnefs renders us liable to the Punifhment threatened to the Tranfgreffors of God's Laws, which would certainly be inflicted upon us, were it not for that full, perfect, and fufficient Sacri-fice, that Chrift Jefus made of himfelf, by which we are told, in the fame Scripture, that he hath obtained eternal Redemption for us ; when (k) *by his own Blood he entered once into the holy Place, having appeared in the End of the World to put away Sin by the Sacrifice of himfelf:* I fay, though Sin (*i. e.* all Sin) is the *Sting of Death,* yet I would not be mifunderftood as if I affirmed or thought, that all Sins were equally offenfive to God in Degree as well as in Kind ; or, that there was no Difference between the Heinouf-nefs of one Sin and another : No, I am far from thinking fo ; for, doubtlefs, without Provoca-tion, wilfully to maim, or cut off a Man's Leg, or his Arm, though it be a very grievous Sin, yet it carries a much lefs Degree of Guilt with it, than premeditately, without Provocation, and in cool Blood, to take away his Life. But what I fhall contend for is, that, though one Sin may be more or lefs heinous than another, and will

(h) 1 John iii. 4.   (i) 1 John v. 17.   (k) Heb. ix. 12, 26.

I 4   there-

therefore (1) *be punished with fewer or more Stripes*; yet, that all Sins are in their own Nature damnable, the least as well as the greatest; agreeable to what St. *James* tells us, when he argues concerning the Breach of the Law; that (m) *he that offendeth in one Point, is guilty of all: For he that said, Do not commit Adultery, said also, Do not kill: Now if thou commit no Adultery, yet if thou kill, thou art become a Transgressor of the Law.* So it is as to other Sins; he that covets his Neighbours Goods, though it be not so much to the Detriment of his Neighbour, is guilty of Sin, and transgresseth the Law of God, as well as he that steals them from him; he that tells a Lie, as well as he that bears false witness against his Neighbour. But, though Punishment is due to every Transgression; yet, being most expresly and frequently assured, in the Scriptures of the New Testament, that (n) *Christ Jesus was manifested to take away our Sins,* that is, the Punishment as well as the Guilt of them; and (o) *was sent into the World, to the End that all that believe in him should not perish, but have everlasting Life;* being made our Advocate with the Father, and the Propitiation for our Sins; we have Reason to hope, that though we have (p) *all sinned, and come short of the Glory of God* (that is, have forfeited the Enjoyment of Heaven, which glorious State God designed for us) yet, that *being justified freely by his Grace, through the Redemption that*

(1) Luke xii. 47, 48.   (m) James ii. 10, 11. (n) 1 John iii. 5.   (o) John iii. 16.   (p) Rom. iii. 24, 25.

is

is in *Chrift Jefus,* and through *Faith in his Blood,* we fhall have *the Remiffion of our Sins that are paft* ; for, as it is (q) *through him that Forgivenefs of Sins is preached, and by him that all that believe are juftified, from what they could not be juftified by the Law of* Mofes ; to which I may add, nor by any other Law : So, our Juftification is not occafioned by the Difference of the Nature of Sins, as if fome Sins had no Guilt, and that therefore no Punifhment was due to them ; but our Juftification is the Confequence of that full Satisfaction that was made for us by Chrift, and of the Merits of his Death, who *(r) was wounded for our Tranfgreffions, and through whofe Stripes we are healed, becaufe the Chaftifement of our Peace was upon him ; who was delivered for our Offences, and was raifed again for our Juftification.*

This Explanation at once gives us all the Hope we can reafonably defire, that from the alone Merits of Chrift's Satisfaction the juft Judgments due to our Sins fhall not be inflicted on us in the next World, unlefs we wilfully perfift in the Commiffion of them ; and at the fame Time deftroys the Notion, that any Sins are venial in their own Nature ; as the Church of *Rome* teaches, who ground their Defence of that Doctrine upon the Words of St. *John,* when he fays, (s) *There is a Sin unto Death, and a Sin not unto Death* ; but this is an Error that has arifen from their miftaking his Senfe ; for the Meaning of that Paffage is not, that fome Sins are mortal, and

(q) Acts xiii. 38 39,   (r) Ifaiah liii. 5. Rom. iv. 25.   (s) 1 John v. 16, 17.

others

others venial ; but that though all Sins are mortal in themselves, yet that some of them will not be so to the Children of God ; because by the Merits of Christ, upon their true Repentance, their Sins will be forgiven them, not being of the Number of those Sins that are unto eternal Death.   I therefore take the true Meaning of that Passage to be ; that by Sins there said to be unto Death, are meant those Sins which are of so deep a Dye, as to have occasioned Declarations in Scripture of their being uncapable of Pardon in the next World ; and that by those which are said not to be unto Death, are meant such as (though very great) are nevertheless not uncapable of Forgiveness in the Life to come ; but not such as are venial in their own Nature, of which the very Notion or Belief is a mere Jest, and a Contradiction in Terms.   Of the former Sort there are two, *viz.* the Sin against the Holy Ghost, and the Sin of Apostacy.   That against the Holy Ghost our Saviour himself has told us, (t) *shall never be forgiven, either in this World or in the other :* And that of Apostacy is represented by the Apostles of our Lord to be uncapable of Forgiveness ; for St. *Paul* tells the *Hebrews*, That (u) *if they who have tasted of the heavenly Gift ; and have been made Partakers of the Holy Ghost, and of the Powers of the World to come ; shall fall away* (that is, fall back to the *Jewish* or Heathenish Worship) *it is impossible to renew them again unto Repentance ;* for Christ having been (x) *once offered to bear the Sins of many,* there re-

(t) Matth. xii. 31, 32.   (u) Heb. vi. 4, 6.
(x) Heb. ix. 28.

mains

mains no more (or further) Sacrifice for the Sins of thofe who apoftatize from Chriftianity, and have thereby *trodden under Foot the Son of God, and counted the Blood of the Covenant, wherewith they were fanctified, an unholy Thing.* And St. *Peter* tells thofe to whom he wrote, That (y) *if after they have efcaped from the Pollutions of the World, through the Knowledge of our Lord and Saviour Jefus Chrift (i. e.* have embraced Chriftianity) *they are again intangled* (turned back to their former Religion) *the latter End muft be worfe than the Beginning, becaufe it had been better for them not to have known the Way of Righteoufnefs, than after they have known it to turn from the holy Commandment delivered unto them;* in as much as by fo doing they reject the Covenant of Grace and Mercy in Chrift. But, as the former of thefe Sins could only be committed by thofe, who attributed the Works and Miracles that Chrift (z) wrought, to the Influence and Affiftance of *Beelzebub,* Prince of the Devils, inftead of believing them to be wrought by the Power or Finger of God; fo the latter of them can only be committed by fuch as forfake the Chriftian Religion, and turn Pagans, *&c.* whofe Repentance is (fo long as they continue in that apoftate State) impoffible to be renewed. From whence it is plain, that they who, at this Time of Day, do fincerely believe, that our Lord and Saviour Jefus Chrift was the Son of God, and who do not apoftatize from his Religion, have no need in the leaft to ter-

(y) 2 Pet. ii. 20.   (z) Luke xi. 15, 20.

rify

rify themfelves with the Denunciations threatened againft thofe Sins which are faid to *be unto
Death*, or unpardonable in the next World ; the
Nature of both which Sins is fo very criminal,
as to occafion the Apoftle's telling the Perfons
he wrote to, that *(a) he did not fay they fhould fo
much as pray for thofe that were guilty of them*.
By the latter, thofe which are faid *not to be unto
Death*, muft be meant all fuch Sins as, though
very great, are neverthelefs capable of being pardoned in the next World, through the Merits of
Chrift, upon our true Repentance ; and are
therefore moft commonly, though not always,
punifhed here by Sicknefs, and other Marks of
God's Difpleafure, inflicted from himfelf upon
Sinners, in order to make them reflect on the
grievous Demerit of Sin, and bring them to a
due Confideration of the Evil of their Doings,
that fo they might avoid the Damnation of Hell,
and by calling their own *(b) Ways to Remembrance* (like *David*) *turn their Feet to God's Tefti-
monies* ; *(c) and by rending their Hearts, rather
than their Garments, might turn unto the Lord ;
who is gracious and merciful, flow to Anger, and
of great Kindnefs, and repenteth him of the Evil*.
For it is natural for People, when they are vifited with Afflictions of any Sort, to remember
the Evil of their Ways, and bring forth Fruits
meet for Repentance, by the Amendment of
their Lives ; in which Cafe God has declared,
(d) That when the wicked Man turneth away from

(a) 1 John v. 16.　　(b) Pfal. cxix. 59.
(c) Joel ii. 13.　　(d) Ezek. xviii. 27.

the

the *Wickedness* that he hath committed, and doth that which is lawful and right, he shall save his Soul alive. When, therefore, we see our Brother fin a Sin that is not unto Death (a Sin not exprefly declared in Scripture uncapable of Pardon) we are obliged, according to the Precept here injoined by the Apoftle (e), to pray for him, that God would fpare him his Life, and give him Space for Repentance, and fhew him his Mercy, not weighing his Merits, but pardoning his Offences, and recovering him to his former State of Health. That this is the Meaning of this Paffage mentioned by St. *John*, may be further gathered from the Context ; for, in feveral Places of this Chapter, he fays, that (f) *he that believeth on Jefus Chrift, is born of God, and keeps his Commandments* ; and that *he that hath the Son, or believeth on the Son, hath Life* ; and that *whofoever is born or begotten of God finneth not, and keepeth himfelf, and that wicked one toucheth him not* ; that is, he that believeth in Jefus keepeth himfelf from finning unto Death, or from being overcome by the Devil to fuch a Degree, as to blafpheme the Miracles of our Saviour, or to forfake his Religion : And, therefore, fhould any Perfon be guilty of thofe Sins unto Death, as (g) fuch Perfon may then well be faid to have made God a Liar, by not believing, or not continuing to believe, the Record that God gave of his Son, and confequently not to have Life ; fo he does not fay (does not injoin) that they fhould

(e) 1 John v. 16.   (f) 1 John v. 1, 3, 12, 18.
(g) 1 John v. 10, 12, 16,

pray

pray for it : But, that fhould any one be guilty of committing fuch Sins as are common, and which, though very great, are not unto Death, being fuch as the Scriptures declare fhall be pardoned upon Repentance, through the Merits of Chrift, he then injoins them to pray for them. This muft be the Meaning of this Paffage, or elfe the Apoftle's Argument, in this and the third Chapter, would prove too much, and confequently be good for nothing : (h) *For, if he that is born of God, or abideth in him, finneth not, or doth not commit Sin ; then whofoever finneth, or doth not Righteoufnefs, hath not feen him, neither known him, nor is born of God, nor is of God.* But, (i) *there is no Man living that finneth not : For if we fay that we have no Sin, we deceive ourfelves, and the Truth is not in us ;* therefore, if whofoever finneth is not of God, no Man living is regenerated, and made the Child of God by Adoption and Grace, or is born of God, or is of God ; and, if no Man living is regenerated, and made the Child of God, then Chrift, who came into the World to fave Sinners, *is dead in vain :* From whence we muft conclude, that the Apoftle does not here mean, that whofoever is born of God, finneth not the common Sins, for which our Saviour is the Propitiation ; but finneth not the uncommon and unpardonable Sins of Blafphemy againft the Miracles of Chrift, wrought by the Operation of the Holy Ghoft ; or that of apoftatifing from his Religion.   There

(h) 1 John iii. 6, 9.—v. 12, 18.—iii. 6, 10.
(i) 2 Chron. vi. 36.   1 John i. 8.

is.

is then no Colour from this, or any other Text in Scripture, whereon to ground the Doctrine of venial Sins; the Belief whereof is of very dangerous Confequence to the Souls of Men: For, were it as true, as it is *falfe*, that fome Sins are of that Nature, yet, as no one whatever, even amongft the moft orthodox of the Church of *Rome*, can, or ever could, exactly tell which they are; or, fuppofing any of them to be fo, whether feveral, or how many of them, may not together amount to fuch a Sin as they call mortal, and ftands in need of the deepeft Contrition and Repentance; or whether the Circumftances attending the Commiffion of them, may not render them damnable, or change them from being venial to mortal; it is certain, that this Opinion tends very much to render us familiar with Sin; fo that by getting the Habit of committing thofe that are efteemed flight ones, we may come to commit thofe that have greater Degrees of Wickednefs in them: For the Boundaries between them, if any at all, being very narrow, they may be eafily paffed over. It is therefore incumbent upon us, from the Danger attending them, not only to avoid the Commiffion of all Sins whatfoever, but even, as the Apoftle directs us, (k) *to abftain from all Appearance of Evil*; and to hold with Proteftants, that, though one Sin may have, and certainly hath, more Guilt in it, and is therefore liable to greater Degrees of Punifhment, than another; yet, that every Sin is, in its own Nature, damnable: The

(k) 1 Theff. v. 22.

dreadful

dreadful Effects whereof we should certainly find, were it not for the Pardon which God, of his infinite Goodnefs, is pleafed to afford to thofe who truly repent of them, for the Sake of his Son Jefus Chrift our Lord. Thus to believe will make us endeavour, with the utmoft Diligence and Watchfulnefs, *to walk in Newnefs of Life*, that (1) *our old Man being crucified with Chrift, the whole Body of Sin may be deftroyed in us*; by which Means we fhall truly lead fuch Lives as the Followers of the holy Jefus ought to live; conformable to his Intention in coming into the world, which was by giving himfelf for us, not only to redeem us from all Iniquity (m), but likewife to purify to himfelf a peculiar People, zealous of good Works. But the Danger of allowing one's felf in the Commiffion of venial Sins, will ftill further appear, if we confider, in Two or Three Inftances, the Difference between the Opinion which the Church of *Rome* has of fome Sins, that are amongft the Number of thofe which they count venial, and the Opinion that St. *Paul* has left us of thofe very Sins. It is a Doctrine of that Church, that venial Sins do not fubject us to the Wrath of God; but Fornication is allowed by them to be a venial Sin; therefore Fornication doth not fubject us (according to their Doctrine) to the Wrath of God. But this is contrary to the Opinion that St. *Paul* had of the Nature of that Sin; for, in his Epiftle to the *Coloffians* (n), he reckons For-

(1) Rom. vi. 6.　　(m) Titus ii. 14.　　(n) Colof. iii. 5, 6.

nication

nication to be one of thofe Sins that fubjected the Children of Difobedience to the Wrath of God ; therefore Fornication cannot be a venial Sin. And, in many other Places of his Epiftles, but efpecially throughout the greateft Part of the Sixth Chapter of his Firft Epiftle to the *Corinthians.* (o), he inveighs againft that Sin, as one of thofe that would exclude the Committers thereof out of the Kingdom of God : And then fays, *That the Body is not for Fornication, but for the Lord ; and therefore God forbid that the Members of Chrift fhould be made the Members of an Harlot* ; and then concludes with bidding them *flee Fornication, becaufe their Bodies were the Temples of the Holy Ghoft.* Again ; fome of the Cafuifts of that Church efteem *Lying* a venial Sin ; though St. *Paul* (p) places it in the Company of *Anger, Wrath, Malice, Blafphemy,* &c. which he commands (q) *to be put* (or left) *off by thofe who feek the Things which are above,* where Chrift *fitteth at the Right-hand of God ; and have put on the new Man after the Image of him that created them.* And, in his Epiftle to the *Ephefians* (r), he directs thofe that have been taught in Jefus, *that they put off the old Man, which is corrupt, and put on the new Man, which is created in true Holinefs,* or (as it is in the Margent) *Holinefs of Truth* ; wherefore *they are to fpeak every Man Truth with his Neighbour.* Further ; others of them maintain, that when Papifts intermarry

(o) 1 Cor. vi. 9, 10, 13, 15, 18, 19.   (p) Col. iii. 8, 9.   (q) Ibid. ver. 1, 10.   (r) Eph. iv. 21, 22, 24, 25.

K   with

with Perfons that then are, or fhall afterwards
turn, Hereticks, the Marriage is void; or at
leaft, that fuch *Romanifts* may leave, or depart
from, the heretical Perfons, and abfent themfelves from their Bed and Board : Though St.
Paul was of another Mind; for he thought that,
in Matters of conjugal Duties (s), neither of the
married Couple had any Power over their own
Bodies, without the Confent of the other; much
lefs that they might feparate from one another,
becaufe of their not being Believers; and he
gives a Reafon why they ought to continue together, becaufe, they might perhaps *fave* (that
is, *convert*) one another : All the Allowance that
he gives in that Cafe is, that the Perfons left are
not bound to follow the Perfons that fhall feparate from them; which, though a Juftification
of the Perfons left, is none to the Perfons that
fhall fo leave them. Thus you fee the Difference between the Judgment of St. *Paul*, and
that of the Church of *Rome* in thefe few Inftances; and I believe, if the *reft* of the *venial*
Sins, which that Church allows of, were exa-
mined by the Rules of *Scripture*, the fame might
be faid of them too.

The only Thing remaining to be refuted, is
her Belief of Purgatory : But, as that depends
chiefly upon the Doctrine of venial Sins, the
Belief thereof muft of Courfe fall to the Ground;
fince that whereon it is built hath been fhewn to
have been a miftaken Notion, without the leaft
Foundation in Scripture. I fhall not however

(s) 1 Cor. vii. 3, 4, 5, 12, 13, 15, 16.

pass it over so slightly, but shall examine it a little, and observe, That if Christ Jesus, by his Passion and Death, and the full Satisfaction he made for all our Sins, hath obtained eternal Redemption for those that believe in him, and obey his Commands (as we are told in many Places in Scripture that he hath ; and particularly by St. *Peter* (t), *that we were not redeemed with corruptible Things, but with the precious Blood of Christ* ; and by St. *Paul* (u), *that Christ, by his own Blood, hath obtained eternal Redemption for us*) there can be no Reason assigned, why Mankind, who are pardoned for the Sake of the Satisfaction made for them by Christ, should be punished for any (whether determinate or undeterminate) Time in Purgatory ; where the Torments for the Time are held to be as intense, as those which the Damned will suffer in Hell itself. Such a Belief is repugnant to the Honour of Christ's Satisfaction for our Sins, as though our Sufferings were necessary to render the Satisfaction of Christ efficacious to our Salvation : Such a Notion is not only not warranted by Scripture, but is contrary to what the Apostle St. *Paul* (x) tells us, *That we are justified freely by Go d's Grace through the Redemption that is in Christ Jesus* ; that is, not by any Works that we can do, or any Punishment that we can undergo, but freely by the Grace or Favour of God, in Confideration of the Redemption that was procured for us by Christ Jesus. If this be not so, the

(t) 1 Pet. i. 18, 19.   (u) Heb. ix. 12.
(x) Rom. iii. 24.

K 2   Re-

Redemption procured for us by Chrift is far fhort of what the Scriptures tells us it is : For we are told there, (y) *That being juftified by his Blood, we are faved from Wrath through him* ; and that *by the Righteoufnefs of One, Juftification came upon All* ; *it being by the Obedience of One that many were made righteous* ; *as by the Difobedience of one that many were made Sinners.* Since therefore the Doctrine of Purgatory is derogatory to the Honour of Chrift's Merits, and that the Scripture, *which is able* (or fufficient) *to make one wife unto Salvation* ; *and is given by Infpiration* ; *and is profitable for Doctrine, for Reproof, for Correction, for Inftruction in Righteoufnefs* ; *that the Man of God* (not only *Timothy* to whom it was wrote, but any of the Men, or People of God) *may be perfect, thoroughly furnifhed unto all good Works* (z), has faid nothing about it : I fay, fince the Scriptures, which are thus fully fufficient to inftruct us in every Thing neceffary to be believed or practifed, hath faid nothing, not fo much as one Word, of any fuch Place or Punifhment, it muft be looked upon to have been an Opinion taken up in the ignorant or corrupt Ages of Chriftianity, for the Sake only of the Profit accruing thereby to the Priefts, whofe Succeffors find it too profitable ever to part with if they can help it ; for it is owing to the Belief of Purgatory that fuch *immenfe* Sums are yearly received by the Priefts, for the innumerable Maffes that are faid for the Dead of the *Romifh* Perfuafion. The Prophet *Ifaiah* tells us, in his

(y) Rom. v. 9, 18, 19.　　(z) 2 Tim. iii. 15, 16, 17.

Fifty-

Fifty-third Chapter (which is fo exprefs a Prophecy of our Saviour's Sufferings and Death, that,
were we not well affured it was written by that
Prophet, we fhould be tempted to think it rather a Narrative or Hiftory of what had happened, than a Prophecy of what was to come to
pafs) (a) *That he hath born our Griefs, and carried
our Sorrows ; that he was wounded* (or, as it is
in the Margent, *tormented) for our Tranfgreffions,
and that he was bruifed for our Iniquities.* What
can the Explanation of that be, but that he fuffered in our Stead the Punifhment due to our
Sins ? Will God then not be fatisfied with the
Sufferings of his dearly-beloved Son ? But that
we alfo, by our Sufferings in Purgatory, muft
add to the Merits of the Atonement and Satiffaction that he made for us ? But this is more
fully expreffed in the following Words : (b) *The
Chaftifement of our Peace* (or of our Pardon) *was
upon him, and with his Stripes we are healed ; we
all like Sheep have gone aftray, and the Lord hath
laid on him the Iniquity of us all.* Hath God
then laid on him our Iniquity ? our guilt ? And
is not his Sufferings and Satisfaction fufficient,
without inflicting, after Death, the Punifhment
thereof upon us in Purgatory ? *The Chaftifement
of our Peace,* or Pardon, *was upon him ;* but, it
feems, that is not of Merit enough, in the Efteem
of the Church of *Rome,* to free us from the Guilt
of our Sins ; but we muft ourfelves make up
what is wanting, by fuffering the Punifhment
thereof in Purgatory ; unlefs we efcape by virtue

(a) Ifaiah liii. 4, 5.   (b) Ibid. ver. 6.

of the Indulgencies that we may *purchase* from
that Church.   By Indulgencies are to be under-
flood, the applying to us some of the Merits of
the Saints departed, which are treasured up in
the Church of *Rome*, to the Intent that they may
be applied to all such Sinners as can or will buy
them, in order to free them from the Pains and
Punishments they must otherwise suffer in Purgatory ; for out of their great Charity it must
be observed, that they never Part with them for
nothing ! I say, unless we can, or will, purchase
some of those Indulgencies we must be content
to burn in Purgatory ; but if we have Money,
and will part with some of it to the Church, we
may escape : For, though Christ's Merits are not
sufficient to free us from suffering in Purgatory,
yet the Indulgencies granted us by the Church
of *Rome*, out of their Treasury of the Works of
Supererogation of the Saints, are ! So that according to this Doctrine, the Sufferings and
Death of Christ are not alone, and of themselves (without either our own Sufferings in Purgatory, or the Application of the Church's Indulgencies) of Weight enough in the Eyes of
God, or rather of the Church of *Rome*, to obtain the full and free Pardon of our Sins ; although he is said in Scripture, to have appeared
(c) *to put away Sin by the Sacrifice of himself* ; *to
have purchased us by his own Blood* ; *to have borne
our Sins in his own Body on the Tree* : All which
Expressions manifestly shew, that he suffered the

(c) Heb. ix. 26.   Acts xx. 28.   1 Pet. ii. 24.

Punish-

Punifhment due to our Sins ; (d) *That by his one Offering he hath perfected for ever them that are fanctified ; whofe Sins and Iniquities God will remember no more* ; and that *where Remiffion of thefe is, there is no more Offering* (or Satisfaction) *for Sin.* Since then Chrift hath purchafed us, or paid our Ranfom for us ; and hath perfected us by the Offering he made of himfelf ; fince God hath (e) *remitted our Sins, and will remember them no more ; fince they are bleffed whofe Iniquities are forgiven ;* I think I may fairly conclude, there can be no Manner of Reafon to believe, that we fhall fuffer the Punifhments which are threatened by the Church of *Rome,* will be inflicted in Purgatory ; or, that there ever was, or ever will be, fuch a Place, or fuch a Punifhment! The Guilt of Sin is the meritorious Caufe of its Punifhment : But the Guilt of Sin is taken away by the Sacrifice of the Death of Chrift ; therefore, the Guilt of Sin being taken away, there remains no Caufe for inflicting the Punifhment thereof.

As for that Paffage, (f) *of Men's Works fuffering Lofs, and being themfelves faved, yet fo as by Fire,* no Purgation of Souls departed can reafonably be grounded thereon ; becaufe nothing is there faid, throughout the whole Difcourfe, either of the Dead, or of the State after Death ; as well as becaufe the Context, and the Scope of St. *Paul's* Argument, is of another Kind, *viz.* to fhew the *Corinthians,* that it would be as dif-

(d) Heb. x. 14, 17, 18.   (e) Rom. iv. 7, 8. Pfal. xxxii. 1, 2.   (f) 1 Cor. iii. 15.

ficult

ficult for Minifters to efcape Cenfure when their
Doctrines and Opinions are thoroughly confidered, if they fhould prefume to lay any other Foundation of Religion than only Chrift Jefus ; or
fhould dare to build thereon, or add thereto, any
other Doctrines or Opinions than thofe which
Chrift and his Apoftles. have delivered and fet
before them for their Rule and Guidance : I fay,
(g) it would be as difficult for fuch Preachers or
Builders to efcape Cenfure, if they taught any
falfe Doctrine, or mixed falfe Doctrines with the
true, as it would for any Works made of Wood,
Hay, &c. not to be burnt were they fet on Fire ;
whereby, however, the found, unmixed, and un-
corrupted Doctrines, fhould not only not be reproved, but fhould receive the Reward of Commendation, even as other Works which are there
fuppofed to be made of Gold, Silver, &c. fhould
remain unhurt by the fearching Flames.   That
this is the true Meaning of this allegorical Paffage of Scripture, which the *Romanifts* have fo
much miftaken in their Explanation of it, is
plain from hence ; that the Apoftle (h) is not
fpeaking of common Chriftians, but of thofe
who *plant* and *water*, that is, of himfelf, and
of *Apollos*, or any other Minifters who labour
in God's Hufbandry or Building, whom he calls
*the Labourers that are to receive according to their
Labour* ; and of Builders and Mafter Builders,
whofe Works are to be made manifeft, when the Days
wherein they are taken into Confideration fhall

(g) 1 Cor. xi. 11, 12, 13, 14, 15.   (h) Ibid.
ver. 5, 6, 7, 8, 9, 10.

declare,

declare, whether the Doctrines they taught the *Corinthians* (or suppose any other common Christians) who are said to be the Husbandry or Building (not the *Labourers*) of God : I say, shall declare, whether the Doctrines so taught were found or perishable, true or false : If true and found, then they should receive the Reward of Commendation ; if false or perishable, that of Reproof. And further to confirm this, that the Ministers of Christ, and Stewards of the Mysteries of God, were the Persons here alluded to, he tells them, in the next Chapter, (i) *That he had transferred this Matter by a Figure* (*i. e.* by this figurative and allegorical Manner of alluding to *Works* and *Workmen*) unto himself and to *Apollos* (that the *Corinthians* might learn not to esteem either of them more than they ought, but only as the (k) Ministers or Stewards of Christ, or hold to the one against the other) in order to put an End to those Divisions and Contentions which he had blamed in them from the Beginning of his Epistle.

But though I utterly deny, that the least Syllable, as I said before, is here spoken of the Dead, or of the State after Death ; I will, nevertheless, for Argument's Sake, suppose, that this Passage has Reference to the Dead, or to the State after Death. Surely, it will by no Means follow from thence, that the Fire there spoken of should be taken for a purgatorial Fire ? Why might it not rather be taken for that of the general Con-

(i) 1 Cor. iv. 6.   (k) 1 Cor. i. 10, 12.

flagration ?

flagration? And then the Explanation might be
thus: That whatever Pollutions the Bodies and
Souls of Men had contracted in their Life-time,
by the false Doctrines they had taught, the wrong
Opinions they had followed, or the sinful Practices they had committed, should be destroyed,
and suffer Loss, even as Wood, Hay, &c. by
that fiery Conflagration: But that whatever Honours or Esteem they had merited by teaching,
believing, or practising such good Doctrines, Opinions, or Practices, as were conformable to the
Foundations laid by Christ and his Apostles,
should suffer no Loss, but like Gold and Silver,
which are not to be destroyed by Fire, should
remain unhurt by that general Conflagration,
and should receive the Reward of Commendation at the Resurrection unto Life.

Further, the Notion of a purgatorial Fire is
contrary to several Passages in Scripture, which
plainly determine, that there is no State of Trial
or Satisfaction after Death. (1) *Blessed are the
Dead which die in the Lord, that they may rest
from their Labours, and their Works follow them*;
the good Works which they did, whilst they
were here in this Life, which is the only Place
of Probation, shall meet with the Praise and
Commendation promised by our Saviour, of (m)
*Well done, good and faithful Servant, enter thou
into the Joy of thy Lord*; and, *Come, ye blessed of
my Father, inherit the Kingdom prepared for you
from the Foundation of the World*: The Faith and
good Works which they professed and practised,

(l) Rev. xiv. 13.   (m) Matt. xxv. 21, 34.

shall

shall be imputed unto them by him who is their Judge, and in whom they are said to die, and through whom they are blessed; and are said to rest from their Labours: But Purgatory is held to be a Place of Torment, not of Blessedness, therefore they that die in the Lord, shall not go into Purgatory. St. *Paul* says, (n) *We must all appear before the Judgment seat of Christ, that every one may receive the Things done in his Body, according to that he hath done, whether it be good or bad:* So that our Rewards or Punishments will be according to what we have done in the Body, that is, in this Life; not according to what Punishments we may suffer in Purgatory after Death. And again he says, (o) *That God will render to every Man according to his Deeds; to those who by patient Continuance in Well-doing, seek for Glory,* &c. *eternal Life; but Indignation and Wrath upon every Soul of Man that doeth Evil.* It is therefore what they have done in this Life; and not what they may suffer in Purgatory; that will determine Mankind's being placed in eternal Bliss, or consigned over to eternal Misery.

I think I have now considered every Article mentioned in the Postscript to your Letter of the 24th of *August*, 1725, relating to your Wife's Belief; and will only add, that I have not, to my Knowledge, said any Thing of the Practices of the Papists, but what I think they are guilty of; or of their Principles, but what I am satisfied may be either directly proved upon them, or fairly deduced from their Tenets; nor made

(n) 2 Cor. v. 10.   (o) Rom. ii. 6, 7, 8.

use

ufe of any Argument againft them, but what I
think is juft. And I hope your Spoufe will either
read this Letter herfelf, or hear you read it, with
all that Serioufnefs and Attention that a Matter
of fo great Moment requires; and I cannot help
fancying, that there are fome Things in this very
long Epiftle (which fhould not have been fo tire-
fome, had I been in a Place that would have allowed me to fhorten it) that are fet in fo juft a
Light, as it is almoft impoffible fhe fhould ever
have had the Opportunity of knowing before;
for which Reafon I hope they will be of fome
Service to her.

I am extreamly glad to find, by what you
fay, that fhe is eafy whenever you talk to her
of thefe Things: I do affure you, my Dear, that
I fhall always pray to God for her Converfion,
with the greateft Serioufnefs imaginable; and
heartily beg of him, that he will be pleafed to
enlighten her Mind with the Knowledge of his
Truth.

I fent you, by the *London*, three Books relating
to the Popifh Controverfy, which I hope you have
received long before this. One of them, intituled, *The Religion of Proteftants a fafe Way to
Salvation*, formerly written by the great Mr.
Chillingworth, is, I think, extreamly well writ,
and the Controverfy very logically difcuffed, and
requires a very clofe Attention, for which Reafon
I fend it you for your own Study. The other
two are, one of them, *A Difcourfe between two
Proteftants*, written by Mr. *Rowlett*, Author of
the facred Poems you ufed to learn by Heart,
when you was young. The other is intituled,

A Pre-

A Preservative against Popery, written by the late Dean *Sherlock*, Author of the Difcourfe upon Death and Judgment; both thefe I make a Prefent of to my Daughter.

I fhall conclude this Letter with the Words of St. *Paul* to the Elders of the Church at *Ephefus*, a little varied; (p) Watch, and remember that during all the Time of your being with me (and fince that by Letters) I have not ceafed to warn you; and now I commend you (and your Wife) to God, and to the Word of his Grace, which is able to build you up, and to give you an Inheritance amongft all them that are fanctified. I am,

Dear G E O R G E,
Your moft affectionate Father,
And fincere Friend,
At Sea, April
15, 1727.   N A T H A N A E L T O R R I A N O.

(p) Acts xx. 31, 32.

P O S T S C R I P T.

I THOUGHT it neceffary to add fomething by way of Poftfcript to this Letter, in order thereby to bring to Light fome other Errors of the *Romifh* Church, which my Father, I find, had omitted; and firft of their Worfhip.

Which muft be in an unknown Tongue; as appears by the Council of *Trent*, Seff. 22. c. 8. and Can. 9. where every Man, who fays it ought
to

to be in the vulgar Tongue, is accurfed. Then the Objects of their Worfhip are Angels, Saints, and the Virgin *Mary*; to whom they pray abfolutely *, and not only mediatively, as they pretend, as appears by their Child's Catechifm in 1678, fo called; where they, praying to a Guardian Angel, fay, "Defend me this Day from all "Dangers, I befeech thee, and direct me in the "Way I ought to walk."

Such as this too is their Prayer to St. *Agnes*, in the *Paris* Miffal, 1520; thus, "O *Agnes*, "Woman of the Lamb, do thou enlighten us "within. Deftroy the Roots of Sin. O ex- "cellent Lady, after the Grievances of the "World, do *thou* tranflate us to the Company "of the Bleffed."

As to the Wood of the Crofs, they not only afcribe peculiar Virtues to it, but they likewife pay to the Wood *direct* Worfhip, by Adorations, Kiffings, Proftrations and Prayers directly to it, to increafe Grace in the Godly, and to blot out the Sins of the Guilty. Nay further they give *Latria* to it, which is fovereign Worfhip, and due to God only. *Pontif. in Bened. novæ Crucis.*

Such is the Worfhip paid to the Hoft; and near to this, that which they pay to Relicks.

As to their Sacraments, they hold thofe accurfed, who do not allow Seven. *Counc. Trent,* Seff. 7. Can. 1. And as to thofe who officiate, they muft have Intention, or the Act is nothing, there is no Sacrament given or received. *Ibid.* 7. 11. So that in this Cafe none can be certain about the Intention of the Prieft, and confe-

* This was hinted at before, Page 32.

quently

quently uncertain, whether they receive or not: Nay, I say further, if the Prieft then adminiftering have never fo good an Intention, and the Prieft who him ordained, had no Intention, he is no Prieft, and his Sacrament no Sacrament, becaufe *Orders* are one of thofe feven Sacraments, in which it is required, that the Intention of the Prieft fhould be to make it valid to the Ordained. —As to Baptifm, they have a particular Form of Exorcifm for the Child, and the Salt which is to be put into the Mouth of the Child * ; with feveral other Things too tedious to be here noticed †.

They deny the People the Cup in the Eucharift ; *firft,* Left it fhould be fpilt upon the Ground ; 2*dly,* Left by being kept for the Sick it grow eager ; 3*dly,* Becaufe many cannot bear the Tafte of Wine ; 4*thly,* Becaufe in many Countries there is fuch a Scarcity, that it cannot be had but at great Expences and long Journies ‡ ; 5*thly,* To difprove (or prove in the wrong) thofe who deny Chrift to be contained under each Species—Which they do, and fay, that in them both and each are, jointly or feverally, truly, really and fubftantially contained, whofe Chrift, God-Man, Body and Blood, Bones and Nerves, Soul and Divinity. *Rom. Cat.* Par. 2. c. 4. n. 33. *Counc. Trent,* Seff. 13. c. 1. *de Real. Pref.* Now

---

* Sure one would think they intended to poifon or choak the Child — *and no doubt it would, if it was not for their* NOTABLE *exercifing it.*

† See *Williams's Romifh* Catechifm, 1713.

‡ And in fuch Cafe the Prieft would not have enough for himfelf.

let

let any one judge, whether this be agreeable to the exprefs Command of Chrift, *Matt.* xxvi. 27. *Drink ye* ALL *of this*; and yet if there is any who fay thefe are not juft and weighty Reafons for denying the People the Cup, fuch are to be accurfed, by the Council of *Trent*, Seff. 21. c. 1. And yet fo far are they themfelves from believing that whole Chrift, *&c.* is contained in either Bread or Wine feparately, that the Reafon they themfelves in their Canon Law, in relation to Confecration, give, why *the Priefts* muft not receive the Body without the Blood, is, becaufe the Divifion of one and the fame Myftery cannot be without Sacrilege.——Such and many more Abfurdities are they guilty of; in this and many other Ways are they felf-condemned, whilft they thus deliver their foolifh Traditions, as Doctrines to be believed and practifed; but they err greatly, *not holding the Head (Col.* ii. 19.) for Chrift never taught one fingle Doctrine as they teach it, and hold it as neceffary to Salvation.

I fhall add no more by way of Poftfcript; but beg Leave to refer my Reader to (and recommend his Perufal of) thofe admirable Difcourfes againft Popery, preached by many of the Diffenting Clergy at *Salters-Hall* in 1734-5; in one of which he will fee, collected from the Scriptures, a moft appofite Defcription of the Church of *Rome*, that Man of Sin, and Son of Perdition *.

* See *Chandler's* Supplemental Sermon, *Jan.* 22, and 29, 1734, Page 53, 54, 55, 56.

LETTERS,

MORAL and ENTERTAINING,

ON

DIFFERENT SUBJECTS.

Quos Tangit Tangat.

SOME

SOME

HINTS

ON

EDUCATION, &c.

IN

A Familiar LETTER from CHRISTIANUS, a Country Gentleman, to his Friend TIMOTHEUS.

Ut Clavis Portam, sic pandit Epistola Pectus.

29th April 1753.
From my own Apartment in the Country.

Dear TIMOTHEUS,

I SHALL not now anſwer your moſt agreeable Epiſtle on the Subject of *Retirement*, which was duly received, from an Inclination I have to acquaint you, that I have endeavoured in this my Neighbourhood, as much as in me lay, according to your Deſire, to inquire into the Truth of the Complaints made by the Lady *Dominica* *, of a very ancient and reputable Family

* Lady *Dominica*'s Story reminds me of the City deſcribed *Eccleſ.* ix. 15, 16. wherein was found a

mily, now almost extinct. I find she has once before made an Application to Mr. *R—r*, who not being successful in his Attempts for her, she applied to me, and, by what I find, has visited these Parts as often as any other, and that upon the Whole, by her own Report, every one has flighted her, and she seems to think her offering herself even as an upper Servant, in any of the *great Families* here, will be a very fruitless Attempt.

Dame *Sanctimonia*, she tells me, advises her against this *Utopian* Scheme, and says she is sure Every-body would think her but a Sort of *Supernumerary*, or a Burden on their Hands.

Being still unsatisfied, and thinking her Defence a proper Work ; in order thereto, I allotted Part of *Passion Week* to make some neighbouring friendly Visits, and indeed, if possible, to know the Truth as to Particulars ; for I have long known her Complaints of a *general* ill Treatment to be just enough, and the Suspicions of *Sanctimonia* still more so ; in consequence whereof, it is impossible she should be approved of by any of these Gentry.

I expected even for Fashion Sake, if nothing else, I should have met with Somebody at Home this Week ; but when I called at Lady *Roley Poleys*, I found she was just going in her Coach and Four, with as many *Loobies* behind, to make

poor *wise Man*, who by his Wisdom saved the City ; yet no one regarded the *poor wise Man* ; and so it is with her, with whom none can be intimate without Improvement.

make up a Party with Lady *Commerce* in her new *Rout Room:* From thence I attempted to drink a Difh of Tea with the young Dutchefs Dowager *D'Ombre*, but was told by the Servant, who has juft quitted her Service on Account of her not being now able to play at Cards more than Five Days in the Week (omitting *Wednefdays* and *Fridays*, on Account of a fevere Penance laid on her, for fome Mifdemeanor, by her ghoftly Father, who knew he could not punifh her more); that *her Grace* had juft had a Fit of *Hyfterics*, and to cure it was gone to amufe herfelf with a *fnug Party* of only Five Tables, at the Countefs of *Quadrille*'s, where I heard afterward there was an Appointment of a large Party made, to go the very next Day to Signor *Quaverino*'s, to hear fome of his favourite Airs; and, that the only Lamentation on this Head was, left there fhould be lefs than *Six* Tables at Cards, or Supper fhould be ready before Eleven: Should the firft of thefe dire Misfortunes happen (or rather to prevent its Poffibility) Mrs. *Schemewell* propofed as a *Succedaneum*, to take up by the Way a few of the beft Cits they could find, that were *tolerably converfable*; but for the laft declared there was no Remedy.

The Five next Ladies I went to vifit were all at Home, but *politely* denied; and, as I found afterwards, Three of them went with Mr. *Deift* or *Atheift* (I knew not which they told me) to the *Orator's Chapel*, and the other Two were bound with *Jack Puppet* for the *Mafquerade*, where by-the-bye they met with another terrible Difappointment, through Mafter's having

L 3 forgot

forgot there were none exhibited in *Lent*, and so were forced, at last (to get rid of Time) to take up with what little Diversion Signor *Timbertoe* could give them, at the *Old W———n's O——t——y.*

After these Attempts, I went home *very tired indeed*, where I met our poor Friend *Dominica*, just come in before me : So, after having entered a little upon the Business she came about, I assured her I could answer for one Friend besides myself (meaning you) whom she might depend on, and be assured we would not see her absolutely want, but help her to the utmost of our Power (which was but little) and, as much as in us lay, recommend her to our best Friends. Upon this she returned pretty well satisfied to her own Chamber (for she lodged at my House that Night) where I shall let her rest, if *Morpheus* will, for a whole Week, and say no more about her, but go on to tell you what I did when she was gone.

I then took up for an Amusement (according to her Desire and Advice, in consequence of our joint Opinion, and in order also to ease myself of the Pain the sympathizing with her Afflictions gave me) that antiquated, obsolete, and now much-disused Book called the *Bible* ; and, as I generally read in most Books (but especially that where all is sacred and divine) wherever I first open (like those who believe the Notion of the *Sortes Sanctorum*) it happened to turn out the 20th Chapter of *Ezekiel's* Prophecy, by the 25th Verse of which I was unavoidably led into the following Reflections, which I have

com-

committed to Writing, together with the above Account, in order to communicate to you. The whole Verse runs thus: *Wherefore I gave them Statutes which were not good, and Judgments whereby they should not live.* On reading which I could not help observing, that when the People of *Israel* had, by many repeated Provocations, offended the Almighty, and, by their multiplied Transgressions, had wearied out his Goodness; *then,* and *not till then,* it was, that *He gave them Statutes which were not good, and Judgments whereby they should not live:* ——*Then,* and *not till then,* it was, that *He gave them up to their own Hearts Lusts, and let them follow their own Imaginations,* Psal. lxxxi. 12; and unhappy must every People be, when this is the Determination of God against them; whenever this happens to be their melancholy Situation, that *He by whom Kings reign, and who teaches Senators Wisdom,* shall, either mediately or immediately, suffer *a strong Delusion, and the Belief of a Lie,* to poison the Morals, debauch the Minds, and subvert the Judgments, of either Prince or People; *when their Teachers shall be removed into Corners, so that their Eyes shall not see them,* Isa. xxx. 20.

The Mind of Man uninstructed is like a Field without Culture, and will infallibly bring forth nothing but Weeds; and yet, so capable is it of Tillage, that, under *proper Tutors and Directors,* it will very readily imbibe the best Principles, as being most natural to the well-tempered Soul.

L 4   It

It therefore concerns every Parent foon to begin that pleafing Tafk of building up the Man.

What! fhall the Florift highly pride himfelf in the fineft Bloom of fading Flowers, and rejoice like the *Olympians* at having gained a Prize, on Account of fome excellent Productions in the Field of Vegetation? And fhall it be lefs Matter of Joy, to accomplifh a rifing Genius in the Field of Wifdom? What! fhall the induftrious Hufbandman rejoice over the pleafing Profpect of a plenteous Crop *, more than he, who by proper Cultivation, has the ftill more happy Profpect of raifing up a beautiful Plant in the rational Field? And, if this is the Duty of every Parent fo to inftruct his Child, that the Ways of Religion and Virtue may be to him *Ways of Pleafantnefs*, and the Paths of Uprightnefs and Juftice, in regard to Morality, *Paths of Peace,* Prov. iii. 17. If, I fay, it behoves every Head of a Family thus to act, in order that he may have fome one to depend upon when he is no more, who will teach his Children after him, *Gen.* xviii. 19. If it is thus incumbent on every Parent to endeavour, as much as in him lies, to ftem the Torrent of Infidelity, Prophanenefs, and Irreligion, and even like *Jofhua* (ch. xxiv. ver, 15.) *to ftand alone in the Service of his God ;* of how much more Confequence is it, confidered in a national Light, that his Education (that of a P—e for Inftance) on whom the future Welfare of many Kingdoms in Ages hereafter may depend, fhould be agreeable to the divine Will? That *the Statutes taught him fhould be good,*

* When the Folds are full of Sheep, and the Vallies ftand fo thick with Corn, that they laugh and fing.

and

*and the Judgments of his Teachers such, whereby
he should live!* That he should be taught to shine
with the greatest Refulgency, whose Influence
must irradiate a prodigious Circle, through whose
Example nothing less than *the Spread of Christianity*, or on the contrary, *a Contagion of Vice*
may intirely depend!

Solomon says, *Ecclus.* xxx. 3. *He that teacheth
his Son grieveth the Enemy*; that is, he enables
such a Son to get the Conquest over him, and
by his own, and the Wisdom of his Counsel-
lors, to be a Victor in the Field; nor is it less
true of the *great Enemy of Mankind* (1 Pet. v. 8.)
who goeth about, seeking whom he may devour: Nor
will any be able to cope with his Wiles and In-
sinuations, but such who have on *the Armour of
God*, and the *Sword of the Spirit* (Eph. vi. 17.)
None will be able to counteract his Schemes, or
have sufficient Force to resist his Assaults, but
such who shall have a *Fortification* raised on virtuous Principles, and whose *Wall of Brass* is a
conscious Innocence.

When King *Solomon* was very young, he was
called, by the Death of King *David* his Father,
to sway great *Judah's* Sceptre, to rule over a
numerous, and no less rebellious People; and
extremely sensible was he, how great the Weight
of Government was to a young Mind, and of
how much Consequence his every future Action
would appear; nor was he less sensible how
weak the unassisted Powers of Man are, and
how absolutely necessary the Direction of God
would be to the well-governing the People committed to his Care, and therefore makes his Petition to his God; but for what? not for *Wealth*

or

or *Riches*, not for *Grandeur* or *Power*, no, nor
even for Victory over his Enemy, or Conquest
in Battles, but for *Instruction in Righteousness*, for
Wisdom and Knowledge, whereby he might PRO-
PERLY *go out before so great a People* (2 Chron.
i. 12. 1 Kings iv. 30). And what was the Result? His Prayer was heard; and as he first ask-
ed for the best of Gifts, and thus was seen *first
to seek the Kingdom of God and his Righteousness*
(Luke xii. 31.) all the rest were added unto him.
Hence we may conclude, that the Instructions
of *David* his Father (1 *Chron.* xxviii. 19.) had
been such Statutes as were good, and the Judgments of the Teachers he appointed for him,
Judgments whereby he should live.

Again: When God declares for a People's
Offence, that *He gives them Statutes that are not
good*, it is (as I apprehend) only meant *permis-
sively*, as a Judgment for their Iniquity, in rejecting him for their God, and not forcibly, so
as to take off the *Culpability* of a People, or
make himself to seem severe in his Dispensations:
And as God never is the first to reject his People
till they reject him, so it greatly behoves us in
this Nation to take heed to avoid a Rejection of
God and his Laws, lest we should be punished
by the Curse of *Zoan* (Isa. xix. 13.) *and a Fool
should reign over us in time to come*, through his
having been taught Statutes which are not good,
&c.

For I greatly fear, we may too justly draw a
Parallel between the *E——h* Nation and the
revolting *Israelites:* God has (through his continued Mercy, and kind unpunishing Delays) set
- over

over us one of the best of Kings, as he did over them, for a great while, one of the best of Prophets, yet they were rebellious and discontented, disobedient to their Prince, and envious at other Nations: And are not we the same? After *Saul*'s Death, *David* was made King, and in his Days the People had the pleasing Prospect of a young *Solomon* to fill the Throne of *Judah*: And are not we equally blessed, who, whilst we *joyfully* view our gracious Sovereign still in Health of Body, and enjoying (and exerting for our Good) every intellectual Power in Perfection, can also see a Prince formed by Nature for a *Solomon*, a Prince fitly qualified to wield the weighty Sceptre, and hereafter likely, by his own Example, to save a sinking Land: A Land sinking in Infidelity and Prophaneness, Excesses, and Debaucheries of all Kinds; a Land vicious, I had almost said (were it not for its numerous and extensive Charities) upon a Par with the *Abominations of the Nations round about us.*

Such then (to go on with my Simile) is our present joyful Prospect of Peace and Happiness, whilst our *David* reigns amongst us; such our Hopes whilst we are blessed with him; namely, that Religion may flourish and abound amongst us; such too is our future Prospect in our all-promising P——e, that, when the People in general shall mourn their King's Demise, then a *Solomon* shall spring up to fill the Royal Seat.

But alas! however formed he is by Nature, however prone to Good, how susceptible soever of the best Impressions; yet in vain may we boast our Prospect, in vain may we raise our
Hopes,

Hopes, if his (yet young and tender) Mind is not watched with the utmoſt Vigilance, and his budding Manhood tended with the greateſt Care.

If his Mind is left uncultivated, we ſhall by and by find it (though no Fault of his own) *like the Field of the Sluggard, and the Vineyard of the Men void of Underſtanding : It will ſoon grow over with Thorns, and Weeds will cover the Face thereof,* when the *Murus Aheneus* ſhall be broken down.

The Liberty of the Preſs is a glorious Liberty ; but I am ſure it is now-a-days groſly proſtituted and abuſed, whilſt few Books, comparatively ſpeaking, can get a Vend that are virtuouſly inſtructive, and whilſt it is made, as it were, a Conduit-pipe for all Manner of Filthineſs, poured through it from the Pens of thoſe who, like *Goliahs* in Infidelity [*], ſeem to defy the Armies of the living God ; thoſe Armies of Divines [†], properly ſo called, and thoſe Nobles, or others, who act the Part of *Laick Divines* [‡], in the Defence of God and his Truth ;

and

[*] *Woolſton, Rocheſter,* and a too long *et cætera.*

[†] See that divine Diſcourſe of the Biſhop of *Norwich :* Wrote on Account of his Highneſs the P—e of *W—s,* and P—e E——d.

[‡] See *Lock* on Human Underſtanding.
———— ———— Education.
———— ———— *Paul's* Epiſtles, *&c.*
See *Woolaſton's* Religion of Nature delineated.
See a Diſcourſe on Providence, no Name.

See

and who endeavour, by their rational Arguments, and the Genteelnefs of their Language,
by the Nervoufnefs of their Expreffion, and Propriety of their Sentiments, to prove that the Religion we profefs (I mean the Proteftant Religion) is a reafonable Scheme ; a Scheme every
Way calculated to fatisfy the Mind here, and
at the fame Time open to us a Door of abfolute
Certainty (founded on the Revelation of the God
of Truth) in regard to the Things which belong
to our everlafting Peace.

In this Religion, and by the propereft Means,
may our P——ce (as no doubt he will) be educated ! Not in the Stupidity of *uncomfortable*
Infidelity, or Bigotry of *Romifh* Juggling ; not
in the Libertinifm of the Age, which is nothing
but Licentioufnefs, nor in the impolitic Policy
of *politely* rejecting his God for his King, or his
Saviour for his God, becaufe perhaps he may be
taught fo, fhould he ever fee it, in the *improper
School for Man* *.

May his Teachers replenifh his Royal Mind
with every Princely and Chriftian Virtue ; may
they adorn it with Graces equal to the Large-
nefs of its comprehenfive Capacity, the Part he

See *Paul*'s Converfion : In a Letter to *Gilbert
Weft*, Author of the Treatife on the Refurrection,
which fee.

See Paraphrafe on *Ifaiah*'s Prophecy, by *Bedding-
field*.

See *Parfon*'s Chriftian Directory.

With many more of both Sorts, which would
make a Volume only to enumerate.

* A Book lately come from *France*.

is

is to act on the Stage of Life; and their own
Abilities to fo important a Charge; then will
the *Robe* and the *Diadem* be but fecondary Ornaments to his Royal Perfon hereafter, and only
ferve (in the Room of fome petit Foible) as a
Foil to his inimitable Accomplifhments.

In order to his being a good and great King
(I humbly prefume) it is not neceffary that he
fhould be brought up in the *Spirit of Fear* : No,
but rather in the *Spirit of Power, of Love, and
of a found Mind* : Not in the *Spirit of Fear*, becaufe our Religion has in it no *Bulls*, no *Ana-
themas*, no perfecuting *Inquifitions*; nothing in
it terrifying or affrighting; but, on the contrary, indulges us in every innocent Amufement,
and every harmlefs Joy; and his being brought
up in the *Spirit of Power*, will enable him to
exert that Power as *Defender of our Faith*.

His being brought up in the *Spirit of Love* will
give him fuch a Love to his Religion, that he
will foon feel how eafy *the Yoke*, and how *light
the Burden* of Chriftianity is; and his being
educated in the *Spirit of a found Mind* will help
him to difcern the Reafonablenefs, and fee the
Beauties, of his Religion, which will not then
proceed from *Bigotry* but *Reafon*.

The Religion of the MESSIAH will bear the
Teft of the ftricteft Examen, and in that to inftruct him will be to give him Statutes which
are really good; and thus to educate him will
prove, that the Judgments of his Teachers are
Judgments by which he may live : This performed with Fidelity and Care (as there needs
no Sufpicion of the contrary) will, in time to
come,

come, make our HEZEKIAH to be to us a *Hiding-place* from the Wind of falfe Doctrines, an Enemy to dangerous Publications, a Covert from the Tempeft of Prophanenefs, and a Meridian Sun to difperfe the Clouds of Idolatry.

How too will fuch an Education as this alleviate the Minds of all true Lovers of their Country, under the affecting Reflection on the Death of our late P———e! How will it fupport them under that Anxiety, otherwife infupportable, which muft fill every Breaft at that Time, when (may the Day be far off) our prefent gracious Monarch fhall be convened to *the Affembly of the Juft made perfect*, and be permitted (as a Punifhment to us, though a Reward of his Labours for us) to change this his *corruptible and fading Crown* for one which never fhall decay, and this his *Kingdom, which is made with Hands,* for one whofe *Builder* and *Maker* is GOD! Then to fee his every Royal Virtue renewed in him, and our King himfelf, as it were, eternalized to his People.

How, laftly, will fuch Inftructions quadrate with her Royal Mind! How joyous will the Profpect be to her (whofe Heart is ever anxious, and whofe Bowels are, as it were, continually yearning after him) whilft fhe fees that *thus inftructed*, his Power and Wifdom do not only make him a *Friend*, but that his Goodnefs and Religion too render him even a kind of GOD to MAN.

Great are the Troubles, and many the Temptations, incident to a Throne; and their Minds
ought

ought to be well riveted in the beſt Principles,
who are to be ſubject to the *Flattery* of every
Perſon about them, and whoſe Situation generally debars them from hearing the Truth.

How ſoon will the Principles of Ethics, Phi-
loſophy, or Divinity, be obliterated, unleſs they
have been *ſtrongly* impreſſed, *Line upon Line*, and
Precept upon Precept, upon his Heart, who is to
guide the *Helm* of a State, ſupport the *Majeſty*
of Government, and be fatigued with the *Burden* of political Affairs, both foreign and domeſ-
tic ! How ſoon may the nipping Froſt of Infidelity kill the tender Plant, and the witty Scof-
fers at Religion turn his every ſerious Principle
into Ridicule, by the Sophiſtry of their Arguments, and artificial Contrivances to lay Stumbling-blocks in his Way, unleſs Care is taken to
give a happy Bias to the Prince's Mind whilſt
it is young, and, like the *Molle udum*, ſuſcep-
tible of any Impreſſion !

Theſe Reflections, dear Timotheus, I
thought fit to convey to you, to make what
Uſe you pleaſe of : I hope you will forgive the
Length of the Epiſtle, and, on Second Thoughts,
believe I could not ſay leſs : I ſhall be glad to ſee
you on this Side the Water, where I enjoy my little *Villa* with Content and Liberty, ſuch Liberty
as is more than a Counter-balance for the higheſt
Dignities and Poſſeſſions in the Univerſe ; where
I enjoy my own ſolitary Reflections, endeavouring to convince myſelf, that Nature is content
with a little ; that he is happieſt who has the
greateſt Command over his Paſſions, and that
                                    our

our Defires, properly limited, feldom want their Satisfactions ; or as the Poet expreffes it,

Nature craves little, Grace fometimes craves lefs,
'Tis Avarice, Pride, and Luft, demand Excefs.
                    RAWLET.

And, as you are a Philofopher, I hope this plain Defcription of greater Plainnefs will induce you foon to vifit,

                    Yours affectionately,

                    CHRISTIANUS.

P. S. For my Anfwer to yours on *Retirement,* for my Letter to *Nathan Dan Saddi* the *Jew,* that to *Alcoranus* the *Mahommedan,* and my farther Hints on *Moravianifm,* be pleafed to be referred to my next.

M   CON-

CONSOLATIONS

TO THE

DOUBTFUL.

IN

A LETTER from CHRISTIANUS to
the virtuous and pious AMINTOR.

Ne esto Justus nimium.

Dear AMINTOR,   *April* 29, 1753.

THE last Visit you favoured me with gave
me great Pleasure; more especially when
I consider the Nature of our then Conversation,
which ran upon Things relating to yourself, and
those too of the most interesting Nature to
you.

The Confidence you put in me (in notifying
to me the History of your Life, from your
younger Years to the present Time, though even
now but young) gave me the highest Pleasure;
and I assure you, I went along with you in your
History Step by Step, in the most sympathizing
Manner; which very Sympathy might be the
very

very Caufe of my now-and-then interrupting you in the Thread of your Difcourfe.

I thought the Vifit, on all Accounts, much too fhort, but efpecially as I fanfied the approaching Evening hurried you home, before you had quite difburdened yourfelf, and that there might remain fomething material to convey to me. If you will forgive me, I will now take my Part in this Affair, and endeavour to fettle you in thofe Principles which you fay you have for fome Time embraced with fuch high Satiffaction : Thofe I mean of the *Chriftian revealed Religion,* thofe *Truths that came by Jefus Chrift.* And the Method I fhall take in fo doing fhall be,

Firft, By recapitulating and anfwering the feveral Charges you made upon yourfelf, and the moft material Things you opened to me about ; and thereby endeavour to convince you, that you have not that Reafon to be diffatisfied with yourfelf, as you have formerly imagined : And then I fhall offer fome Means of Confolation to you from the Holy Scriptures.

The firft Thing you mentioned to me was, I think, a want of a complete Knowledge of the Holy Scriptures, and that too when you was but a Child : Now I would defire you, in this Cafe, to judge for yourfelf, as you would for another. Is it very likely, that the whole Will of God fhould be underftood by a Child, who could not be fuppofed to have had fo many Opportunities of being informed as many have, who perhaps had none about him, who were at all fkilled in *Polemical Difputes?* It is not to be wondered at,

that

that the *feeming* Contradictions in Scripture (and which only can be explained by themfelves) fhould puzzle a young Mind; and the more I affure you it would do fo, the more defirous you were to underftand them; and that for this Reafon, becaufe too eager a Defire takes away, in fome Meafure, our digeftive Faculties, which, efpecially in young Perfons, can be improved but by flow Degrees.

The Uneafinefs you exprefled at the Want of Refolution (tho' you had the Defire) to open your Mind, and receive Inftruction, was to me a convincing Proof, and fure Mark of your Sincerity, and what I believe, and am fure, is the conftant Attendant of a well-difpofed Mind in its Refearches after Truth; and you need not fear, but your earneft Defire to know was accepted of, by him who fees the Heart, for as good a Service to him, as if you had fooner had an Opportunity of fatisfying yourfelf; fince it only came from Bafhfulnefs, or a Fear of being laughed at as too religious : Things very natural to a Perfon of your Age, and Turn of Mind.

The higheft Charge you throw upon yourfelf is your *deiftical Principles*, in believing no revealed Religion; nor no Satisfaction by Chrift; nor no need of this Sacrifice; and, at the fame Time, having a thorough Self-fatisfaction and Eafe.

This Charge, fuppofing it true, is a very heavy one; for it is abfolutely impoffible for us to have a well-grounded Hope, till we have a lively Faith: But I cannot be perfuaded, but
there

there muft have been fomething CONSTITU-
TIONAL in this, or fome unufual Impreffion made
upon your Mind, either by Converfation fimilar
to thefe Principles (the which as you had not
Anfwers ready to confute, fo you gave a kind of
negative Affent thereto) or elfe, perhaps, thefe
Notions might be imbibed from fome Books
which fell into your Hands, which are the fame
as Converfation, only rather more hurtful, becaufe the Stile of Books generally exceeds the
Oratory of moft Perfons.

That the Satisfaction of Mind, whilft in this
State, was conftitutional, I can plainly prove to
you, and that too from your next Obfervation on
yourfelf, which I think was at the Death of your
beloved Friend *Theodoret* ; at which Time you
fay you was fo affected, as to have no Satisfaction
at all in thefe Principles, and to have had a kind
of immediate Turn in the Mind impreffed by
this Affliction ; and this was plainly becaufe the
bodily Organs were differently affected, and, in
confequence, you faw Things in a different Light.
This I take to be the Cafe, and not from any
rational Conviction wrought upon your Mind.
But, however, I will coincide with you, and I
will fuppofe that this Alteration of Sentiments
was the Impulfe of Heaven, that the Death of
your Friend was a Means made ufe of by God
for your Good (for he is merciful in his fevereft
Difpenfations): And even confidered in thisLight,
which I take to be the Light you yourfelf confider it in, you have no Ground of Reflection
upon yourfelf, in regard to your former Notions
and State of Mind ; for it might be the Wifdom

M 3   of

of God, who *createth Evil* to good Purpofes, to
fuffer your Mind to be as it were under *Fetters
and Chains for a Time*, that you might rejoice
the more when you (by the enlightening thereof)
were admitted *into the glorious Liberty of the Children of God*.

This was the Cafe of St. *Paul* ; and as you
(with him) readily embraced the heavenly Sum-
mons, and divine Lights, when it fhone upon
your Mind with a dazzling Luftre, fo you need
not fear but you will be affifted, in the Profe-
cution of your Duty, by the fame *heavenly
Guide* as he was in his Miniftry.

You obferved further, that, at the Time you
were under the Power of thefe bad Impreffions,
you ftill felt a fenfible Love of God, which is
abfolutely inconfiftent with a *Deift*, for this plain
Reafon, That if there was no Revelation there
would want much of that Goodnefs and Mercy
in God which the Difpenfation of the Gofpel
offers : And further ; whoever looks into their
own Natures, and fee the many Defects that are
obfervable in the beft managed Life and Converfation, muft fee fufficient Reafon to fear, that
*fhould God be extreme to mark what is done amifs,
none could abide* ; and that, therefore, unlefs God
Almighty were pleafed to reveal to us a Ground
of Hope, and fhew us a Mediator between him
and us (and that too (as he has done) in a Manner almoft inconceivable) we fhould find ourfelves without *Hope*, and that might make us
think that we were alfo without *God* in the
World ; and this Reprefentation of God to our
Minds muft fix fuch a Fear of him, as is in-
con-

confiftent with *that Love, which cafteth out-Fear.*
This muft indeed introduce Notions of God only
confiftent with a *Deift,* or (I had almoft faid) if
that could be, an *Atheift,* but not of a CHRIS-
TIAN : And therefore I would hence conclude,
that as you found this intire Love to God, you
could be no Deift ; and that it muft have been
a falfe and ill-grounded Accufation of yourfelf,
which proceeded only from conftitutional Impreffions.

The Accufation you lay to yourfelf of Hypo-
crify, in feeming to pray and attend the Ordinances of Religion out of Fear of the World,
was no Matter of Accufation at all ; becaufe,
by your own Confeffion, it was not from Pride,
nor from defpifing the Ordinances themfelves
(that made you unwilling to go ; and that it was
from a religious Fear of hurting others that you
complied with going to them ; which was fo
good a Motive, that it would almoft have warranted you in the Neglect of a Duty on fo charitable an Account ; almoft, I fay, have warranted
you in *doing Evil that Good might come* ; and was
moft certainly the ftrongeft Motive in the World
for you to take Part in the Ordinance of the
Lord's Supper, when you might fo thoroughly
prove yourfelf to be in Charity and Love with
others, which is one of the beft Preparatives
thereto that I know of ; and befides, it is doing
according to Chrift's Commands, who hath faid,
*That whofo doeth his Will, he fhall know of his
Doctrine whether it be of God* ; and therefore
your communicating might be a Means of fet-
tling your affrighted Mind.

M 4   You

You mentioned alfo, that, in order to difburden your Mind, and fet yourfelf free, you were willing to *try* your own *Spirit,* and were determined, at all Hazards, to feek to fome fpiritual Guide for Counfel, that you might go upon fome folid Grounds, and know whether you were, or were not, in the right Way; that in order hereto, you wrote down your then Faith and Belief in the moft exact and fcrutinizing Manner you were able (which, by the way, I would have you always keep by you, that you may now-and-then compare your own Sentiments with themfelves); and that then you fhewed this Paper to *Theophilus,*; that he fully approved of it, and gave you from thence a well-grounded Hope and Confidence towards God, and confequently great inward Peace and Satisfaction of Mind thereupon. Two Things I will beg Leave to obferve on this laft Account of yourfelf.

Firft, That when Reafon took place, you foon got rid of your Bafhfulnefs, and that Fear you had of difcovering the State of your Mind; which, as I obferved above upon that Article, was nothing but the Force of Youth, and conftitutional Fear.

Secondly, You may hence obferve, that you really were a right Believer, though you did not know it; and that may prove to you, how apt pious and well-meaning Chriftians are to accufe themfelves too hardly, nay, even of Things they never thought of, whilft the fanguine People, and Perfons of naturally good Spirits, oft excufe, and forgive themfelves too foon; both which forts of Perfons are but bad Cafuifts for themfelves. The

The very great Uneafinefs you felt in your Mind, upon the Reflection of your want of Faith once, and your preferring any Pains in Body before this Pain of your Mind, was to me a convincing Proof of your great Sincerity ; and it is alfo the conftant Attendant upon unfettled Minds. This great Uneafinefs was a permitted Evil to you, and was in the Hand of God as a Leading-ftring by which he held you, in order to check you when falling, and not a Sign of his having caft you off ; for we are told, *That whom the Lord loveth he chafteneth, and fcourgeth every Son whom he receiveth* ; and, *What Son is there whom the Father chafteneth not ?* And again we are told, *That the Palm-bearing Multitude muft go through much Tribulation.*

As to your having had, as you fay, fome Doubts about the *Athanafian* Creed, that is not to be wondered at, fince I will take upon me to fay, that not ône in fifty that repeat it underftand it ; nor need they, in my Opinion, in order to their eternal Salvation : For it was a Creed founded, as I apprehend, by a Set of Partifans in the Fourth Century of the Chriftian Æra, and was carried to that Heighth of Expreffion, to which it is, as I conceive, merely to counter-act what was then called the *Arian* Herefy : And though, perhaps, it was very proper for the then Purpofe of the Compilers (*who, I fuppofe, thought to drive out one Poifon by another*) yet it never would have been fo conclufive in its Expreffions, had it not been ftrained by religious *Partifans* and *Zealots* of the different Ages through which it paffed, and by which it has received many Alterations.

So

So never trouble yourself about that; for whatever is above us, is nothing to us *; and we may as well suppose we shall be punished for not being able to lift a Weight, which is heavier than ourselves, as for not believing what we cannot comprehend. What you can comprehend, you can examine; and what you understand, you can assent to, or dissent from, as is most agreeable to your best-informed Judgment; and be assured, that a willing Mind is accepted according to our Abilities; that God requires no more of us than he enables us to perform; and if he suffers us to be tempted, he does it for our Good; and *though we fall, we shall not be cast down, for God upholdeth us by his Hand.*

I think I have now gone through all your Accusations; I have now travelled with you through all the rough and rugged Paths, and have, I hope, brought you to a Haven of Satisfaction in your now present Persuasions; all which it is now in your own Power to continue to yourself, by your own consequent Behaviour. I, for my Part, was thoroughly convinced, when I talked with you, that I might justly speak Peace to you (as far as I have any Power of so doing); but I chose rather to do it after I had considered your Arguments against yourself, lest I might seem, from any partial Motive of Friendship to you, to cry *Peace, Peace,* where there was not sufficient Ground of Peace. There is nothing uncommon in your Case at all; nothing

---

* *Quod supra nos est non est nobis*; and yet it does not follow that no Mysteries are to be believed, when they are really such, and not (by implying absolute Contradictions) absolute Absurdities.

but

but what moſt well-meaning low-ſpiritedly religious Perſons are ſubjeſt to ; and therefore I may
apply to you the Words of our Saviour to blind
Bartimen, Your Faith hath made you whole ; *Go
in Peace.*

And now, dear *Amintor,* that you are ſafely
landed, do not be carried away by every *Wind
of Doſtrine,* nor follow thoſe, who, under a ſpe-
cious Pretence of ſhewing you a more excellent
Way, are laying wait to deceive : Do not follow them (left they ſhould prove *thoſe buſy Mock-
ers* ſpoken of, *to come in the laſt Time, who ſhould
walk after their own Luſts, ſeparating themſelves,
not having the Spirit*) ; but be upon your Guard,
and keep ſtedfaſt and immoveable in that Church,
the Precepts of which, when duly obſerved, will
teach you how you may fear the Lord in the
Way moſt agreeable to him ; not in the *ſlovenly*
Way of *Conventicles,* but in the *Beauty of Holi-
neſs,* with ſuch Decency and Care as muſt be
moſt agreeable to him, who is a God of Order,
and not of Confuſion.

Such Places as theſe are not warrantable to be
reſorted to, but in Caſes ſimilar to the apoſtolic
Age, when the primitive Chriſtians had no publick Aſſemblies to meet in but by Stealth, when
the true Worſhippers of God were found to hide
themſelves in Dens, and Caves of the Earth,
and dare not, as we now may, openly profeſs
the Faith of Chriſt, without laying themſelves
liable to Perſecution on that Account.

Reſorting, if you do, to theſe Places, is, in
ſome Meaſure, breaking your Purpoſe, of keeping exaſtly in that Way which you were in
when *Theophilus* approved of your Account of
yourſelf ;

yourfelf; and what is worfe, it is running a
Rifk of being biaffed in your Principles, by following thofe innovating *Fanaticks*, who are but
like a *Glow-worm* in the Dark, who (by your
following only their fpecious Pretences to better
Light, and their fhining Outfide) may lead you
again into fome untrodden Paths, which may
unawares fink you again into the *Mire* of Infta-
bility, and *Chaos* of Uncertainty : For indeed it
feems by thefe Perfons, as if the Time fpoken
of by St. *Paul* to *Timothy* was come, when *People will not endure found Doctrine, but after their
own Lufts heap to themfelves Teachers, having itch-
ing Ears.*

Believe me, dear *Amintor*, they are *Enthu-
fiafts*; believe me, when I affure you, that *Enthufiafm* has done more Harm than *Idolatry* ever
did : Becaufe, *Idolatry* is *vifible Bigotry*, and as
fuch is not fo dangerous as *Enthufiafm*, which,
under a violent Shew of worfhipping God, is
only *mafqued Idolatry*, or the Proftitution of the
reafonable Mind to Chimeras inftead of a Deity,
or to an invented imaginary God : For it is as
much Idolatry to worfhip God in an ideal Way
which cannot belong to him, as it is to raife
Images of his Form or Perfon, and adore them ;
for we are to frame no Likenefs at all of him.

The Mind of Man is an active Principle, and
muft be always employed, and therefore it fhould
be well conducted : It is alfo a weak Principle,
and therefore fhould not be burdened with dif-
putable Queftions, and Strife about Words ; becaufe, that all Things abfolutely neceffary to
Salvation are to be found in the plain and eafy
Doc-

Doctrines of the Gospel of Christ ; and you need look no farther, but read the Scriptures daily ; for they are the Oracles of God, *and are able to make you wise unto Salvation,* and *they are they which testify of God and Christ :* They contain in them an *Anodyne* to every Pain, and an *Antidote* to every *Poison* of Satan.   In them you will find the healing Balsam to a wounded *Spirit,* as well as a *cathartic Potion,* or *amputating* Knife for every Vice ; whereas Books of Controversy on the Mysteries, and abstruse Points of Religion, often tend to the bewildering, instead of settling, the Mind.

The most necessary Thing, in order for the well conducting of our Lives, is the firm Belief of these three Points, which once thoroughly rooted and grounded in us, will make us *perfect, strengthen, stablish,* and *settle us ;* and they are these that follow :

First, The Belief of the Being of a God, or first uncreated Cause.

Secondly, Of his Providence and Superintendency over us and our Affairs.

Thirdly, Of the Redemption of lost Man by Jesus Christ ; and I think we need no other to render us happy here and hereafter.

Because the first of these Principles will naturally lead us to adore him as our CREATOR, to trust in his *Power,* to love him as our *Father, Friend,* and *Benefactor,* in as much as he has given us our Being (and by that a Power of being happy for ever) and every other Blessing we enjoy ; and has provided an Habitation for us, which (when this earthly House of ours shall be

dif-

diſſolved) will be eternal in the Heavens. This
will lead us to pray unto him in all our Wants
and Needs, which may bé fometimes done *ex-
tempore*, but rather by the Aſſiſtance of good
Books ; in as much as they are more correct,
and often more expreſſive of our ſpiritual Wants :
And, in order to keep us up to the Standard of
our Perfection, Self-examination may be fometimes proper, provided it be under proper Regu-
lations ; for otherwife it will be very dangerous
to the beſt People, who very often, for fear of
not confeſſing enough, charge themfelves with a
Load of Guilt which no-way belongs to them,
and, as it were, *lie* to God.

The Uneaſineſs which Infidel Principles give
(which can never be founded upon Reafon, whatever they pretend) are an Argument of the great
Confolation which the Belief in the Being of a
God gives. Nor is the Second Article leſs replete with Comfort ; I mean, his Providence
and Superintendency over us and our Affairs :
For if we confider him as *about our Bed, and
about our Path, and ſpying out all our Ways,* we
ſhall naturally behave ourſelves with a good Degree of Awe and Reverence before him ; and
this will keep us from many Sins, which (for
want of this Perfuafion) we might commit. If
we confider him *as ever with us,* we may then
hope to have *both his Rod and Staff to comfort us.*
When we confider him in this Light, we may
moſt furely reſt ourfelves in him, in all our Ne-
ceſſities, whether they relate to our Bodies, or
our Souls, believing this will lead us to hope for
Victory over Temptations, in Confidence that
he

he that is with us, is greater than he that is in the World; for fo he tells ùs by his Prophet: *Fear not, I am with thee: Be not difmayed, I am thy God*; and where we ftrive, *his Spirit worketh with our Spirit, making us to do the Things that pleafe him.*

This will alfo lead us to a kind of contemplative Converfe with him, when we behold all Nature fupported by his PROVIDENCE, and we ourfelves made fuch Sharers in his *Bounty*, as to be even LORDS of this lower World. But yet, notwithftanding the Force this kind of Obfervation on *Providence* has, we find it infufficient to anfwer all the Purpofes of our prefent and future Happinefs, in as much as it has not fufficient Force to counter-act our Frailties: But then againft thefe we (in the third Point of our Belief, hinted at as neceffary for the Conduct of our Lives) have the Redemption of loft Man by Jefus Chrift, as a full and fufficient Salve for every Sore; the which although there are fome in the World, who (either for want of proper Education, or through the wilful Mifapplication thereof) do not only live as if there never had been a *Meffiah*, or the Son of God, in the World; but alfo who openly deny him, and laugh at every one who profeffes to believe in him: Yet, if we trace thefe Perfons to the Borders of the Grave, to the Confines of Eternity, we then find the Weaknefs of that Reed they lean on, mere human Reafon, and plainly may obferve how glad they would be, could they then embrace, with a well-grounded and religious Hope, the Promifes of God made to us in Jefus Chrift.

Chrift.　And this may ferve as a ftrong Argument to every-one who would wifh to be comforted under the Weight of an uneafy Mind, to fly to this Faith as to *a Fountain of Living Water*, and make them eager *to draw for themfelves out of the Well of Salvation :* This Belief once fixed (which certainly will be fixed, unlefs we throw out all divine Revelation, every Impulfe from Morality, and even thofe firft Principles, which the Light of Nature makes clear to us) ; I fay, unlefs we difcard all thefe, it is impoffible but we muft, by a Train of Arguments, trace out a Redeemer, and *find out the Lamb that was flain from the Foundation of the World :* And if we further admit the Revelation of the written Word, conveyed to us by *Mofes* and the Prophets, we then may find out fuch fure and infallible Teftimony by Types, by Prophecies, by Revelations to good Men, and even Convictions of Infidèls (and afterwards, in the firft Ages of Chriftianity) as are fufficient to take away every the leaft Doubt concerning thefe Things. And this Saying will appear (even to your *highflown Rationalifts,* as well as others) worthy to be received, THAT CHRIST JESUS CAME INTO THE WORLD TO SAVE SINNERS.

Thefe Principles of the Belief of a God, his Providence, and our Salvation by Chrift, once fixed, will appear moft comfortable, in as much as they will be the greateft Support to us under the Evils of this Life, and alfo by them we *fhall have an Entrance miniftered abundantly to us, into the Joys of God's heavenly Kingdom,* WHERE *the Wicked ceafe from troubling,* and WHERE *the Weary*

Weary are at reft ; WHERE we fhall no more be rendered miferable through Anxiety, Uncertainty, and doubtful Reafonings ; but WHERE the gracious SCHEME of our Redemption will tranfcendently appear to be (to us the Exertion) both of the *Power* and of the *Wifdom* of *God.*

I have now but one Thing more to offer in confequence of our Converfation, which is, in regard to your going to the *Spaw* ; a Place you feem to be fearful of for yourfelf : But this Fear itfelf will be your Security ; for there are none fo likely to fall as thofe who fear no Danger. Befides, as you do not go for the Love of the Place, its Gaieties, &c. fo you have, on the other hand, a very warrantable Reafon to go, the Care of your fick Friends, whofe ill Health wants the Affiftance of your good Health : And in thefe Things we are warranted by the Example of our Saviour, who went into the worft Places and worft Company, in order to do Good : And here the Intention fanctifies the Act, as the Altar fanctifies the Gold.

You need not, you know, follow the Diverfions of the Place, fo as to become fond of them ; nor need you cloifter yourfelf up, and wholly abftain from thofe Recreations, which can only be rendered hurtful by Abufe.

And now, my much-loved *Amintor,* I will take my Leave of you, committing you to the Protection of Almighty God ; defiring you will take in good Part every Thing contained in this long Letter, which, in every Article, I could have enlarged upon, would Time have permitted me : More I did not chufe to fay, for fear of tiring you ;

N   and

and lefs I could not fay, confiftent with my
Efteem for you, and the Obligation of Duty I
am under to comfort you, all that is in the
Power of,

Your affectionate Friend,

C H R I S T I A N U S.

P. S. I hope I fhall have the Pleafure to hear
from you from the *Spaw*, where I wifh you a
Continuance of Health and Happinefs, and
that Eafe which your own Mind is capable of
giving you; heartily wifhing, in Confequence
of your pious Life here, you may help to
compofe the Numbers of them who fhall be
God's own, when *he maketh up his Jewels*.
If you find any Expreffion which may appear
unbecoming, I hope you will impute it to nothing but my want of knowing how to clothe
my Thoughts in better Language.

A Mo-

A
Monitory LETTER
from
THEOPHILUS
to the
Unfortunate MAGDALENA.

Be not wicked over-much, neither be thou foolish : Why
shouldst thou destroy thyself before the Time ?

MADAM,

IT is sometimes one of the most *necessary*, tho'
perhaps one of the most *disagreeable* Tasks in
the World, to write to an unknown Person by
an unknown Name, as I must now do to you,
having never seen you, or heard your Name :
But the Necessity of such Epistles appears from
the Nature of their Subjects, and the Disagree-
ableness of writing them from there being such
Occasion.

Now

Now this Letter is one of that Sort, and comes to you as to a Person, who (according to the Information I have had from one of your real Friends, who defired me to write it, as thinking me a proper Inftrument for your Converfion) are one of the moft miferable of all human Creatures, a Woman (a Gentlewoman) abandoned to every Vice, even fo as to glory in her Shame.

I chufe not to enter into a particular Detail of the many Circumftances I have been informed, to complete your unhappy Character, and fhall only mention fome few.

I have been informed that you are married, and that you are a Proftitute; and alfo that you, being pregnant, have endeavoured at unlawful Means to ftifle the little innocent Embrio in your Womb: That prophane Swearing is what you pitch upon as an Ornament to your Converfation, and blafpheming the Name of the Great Supreme one of the Embellifhments which you feem to think fets off the Females Difcourfe.

Now, Madam, as to the firft, That you are married, only confider with yourfelf the Solemnity of your Vow at that Contract; think of your once giving your Hand and Heart to a Perfon, chofe out of the whole Species for the Companion of your future Life; and thence conclude, how indifpenfibly you are obliged to render all your Endeavours ferviceable to the Comfort of your joint Lives! How natural it was to expect an Offspring from the lawful Ufe of the Marriage-Bed; and the Duties confequent thereupon, in regard to your Children;

and

and then reflect, how agreeable is your Conduct to that Part of Duty, while you hate the Children of Wedlock, and think yourself then only happy when you are in Company with your Brute Creatures.

Can this be pleasing to your Husband? Must it not highly grieve him, to think he has placed his Affections so unworthily? And the more he loves, and the less he is able to wean himself from you, so much the more must it grate him to see you render that Person, in which he placed his Felicity, a common Sacrifice to every leud Embrace, and, I had almost said, a common Channel for the vilest Practices.

If this Consideration will not move you, if the Respect due to your Husband has no Force, yet, let even Self-Interest some Way bias you, and consider the Misery of that Distemper which is the just Judgment of God upon the Crimes of Inconstancy, and which, sooner or later, must end in Death; *for the Joy of Fools is but for a Moment.* Consider also (from the same Principle of Self-Love) that whilst you are endeavouring to destroy your Child (whether lawfully or unlawfully begotten matters not); I say, whilst you are endeavouring to destroy that, you do not do less towards your own Destruction; and you may *plunge* yourself into *Hell* sooner than you are aware: But believe me, *it is a dangerous Thing to play with Firebrands, Arrows, and Death, and to say, Am not I in Sport?*

Consider, how neglected must those Children be, whom you are already entrusted with: And Children are the Gift of God, and Talents in

their

their Parents Hands, for which they are accountable; and if you will take no Care of them, you muſt expeſt that their *Blood will be required at your Hands*; and that if you continue to negleſt them, you will be worſe than the rich Man in the Goſpel (who, conſcious of the Miſery he himſelf felt, was deſirous none other ſhould follow his Crimes) in as much as you both give a bad Example, and alſo altogether negleſt Precept, and adviſing them for their Good; the which indeed you could not, with much Reaſon, expeſt ſhould be regarded, unleſs your Precept went hand in hand with your Example.

I muſt tell you, Madam, that you are not in a State of Safety (nor is there any Hope for you in God) without the ſevereſt Repentance, and a thorough Reformation. You muſt forſake your Sins, or be miſerable for ever; for there is no Medium: You muſt not think to bargain with the Almighty, nor muſt you trifle with omnipotent Power. But even ſuppoſe this could be granted you, I do not ſee what you have to plead in Arreſt of Judgment; becauſe I do not find, that, at preſent, there is the leaſt remaining aſtive Virtue left in your Soul, to give to God in lieu of your indulged favourite Vices.

Let theſe Repreſentations of yourſelf to yourſelf have ſufficient Force in them to ſtir you up to ſuch an Hatred of your Sins, as will be productive of good, wiſe, and ſteady Reſolutions of forſaking them; fix in your Mind a Dread of God's Power; impreſs your Soul with the Thoughts of an immeaſurable Eternity of Bliſs

or

or Mifery : And, to encourage you in this defired Change, confider the Goodnefs of God,
who has hitherto fpared you from the Gate of
Death (perhaps on purpofe) that I might have
this Opportunity of fending you this Warning,
and you of receiving it before you die.

Grafp then the happy Opportunity of remaining Life, and delay not for a Moment longer, becaufe there is no Repentance in the Grave, whither we are all, even the moft healthy of us,
hafting apace. Confider, and examine carefully,
the firft Inducements which led you off
from thofe Impreffions which were made by a
good Education : Confider, and reflect with
Grief and Sorrow, upon the Lofs of thofe real
Friends, who were weaned and forced from your
Society by the Profligancy of your Life, and
run in hafte to affure them of your defigned Reformation ; and beg they will aid you therein by
their Counfel and Advice, that they will again
renew their ufeful Acquaintance with you, and,
by that Means, keep you from affociating any
longer with thofe who have been hitherto fo
hurtful to you.

Go to your injured Hufband, and acknowledge yourfelf confcious of the Abufe of his
Goodnefs, but that you have *thought on your
Ways*, that you *have done amifs, and dealt wickedly*, but you will *do it not again :* Go to your
abufed Children, and embrace them anew in
your repentant Arms, and henceforth nourifh
and cherifh them with your moft cordial Affection ; then you will find, that thofe two firft
Steps of Repentance gained, I mean, Confeffion

　　　　　and

and Refolution, the Work will then go on eafy and glib; then you will have Reafon to be fomewhat filled with Hope, which Hope will induce you to apply yourfelf to the Throne of God for the Grace of Perfeverance, which, whilft you are as you are, you cannot expect; for *God heareth not Sinners, but if any one is (or becomes) a Worfhipper of him, him he heareth.*

Tafk yourfelf every Hour of the Day with fomething to fill up your Time, that is at leaft innocent, if not abfolutely neceffary, that fo you may not have any Part of your Time lie idle upon your Hands: And, in order that your Thoughts may have a good Tendency, furnifh yourfelf out of the holy Scriptures with proper Portions, to ufe as Ejaculations, of which you may there find a plentiful Number to fuit every Occafion.

As thus: When you are going to do wickedly, think on God's Omniprefence; that *his Eye is in every Place, beholding the Evil and the Good*; that *he is of purer Eyes than to behold Iniquity*; that *without Holinefs no Man fhall fee the Lord.*

When, by Reflection on your wicked Life, you are almoft ready to defpair, reflect on the *Joy* expreffed to be in Heaven at a Prodigal's Return, where the Father runs out to meet the repenting Son with open and compaffionate Arms.

Thus let me, by the Mercies and Severity of God, move you to Repentance; let me conjure you immediately to fhake off all your Sins, that fo *Iniquity may not be your Ruin:* And, if what I have here wrote has any prefent Influence on
your

your Mind ; if it fhould affect you at the firft but with a Wifh, that your State towards God was otherwise than it is, cherifh the invifible Fire by the Blaft of the afpiring Heart, till it thoroughly kindle into a Flame of Goodnefs. Roufe (and that inftantly) from your Lethargy, and Sleep in Sin, and *rife from the Dead, that Chrift may give you Life,* who never *breaks the bruifed Reed,* nor does he *quench the fmoaking Flax.*

Do not be too much frightened at the amazing Profpect of your guilty Soul, that fo you may not be led to defpair (though you may have great Reafon to fear) ; but rather, let it appear to you as a Storm, which (though for a Time, it makes you almoft at your Wit's End, yet) may, if you do not quit the Helm, hereafter give you the agreeable Senfation of fo ferene a Calm, as will prefent you with a Profpect of that Haven where you would be.

Lay yourfelf open to God without Referve ; and the more fo, becaufe it is impoffible to hide your Sins from him ; for there is no Place fo fecret where he fhall not fee you, nor can the Depth of Darknefs hide you at all from him.

This humble and plain Confeffion you are encouraged to make by him who *came to heal the broken in Heart* ; who came to fet us free from the Burden of our Sins, whenever we are really *weary and heavy laden* with their Weight ; for *whofoever confeffeth and forfaketh his Sins fhall find Mercy.*

You fhould confider that your Sins are of the deepeft Dye ; they are *red like Crimfon,* and
therefore

therefore your Repentance ought to bear some Proportion thereto. It is not a few slight Tears that will intirely answer the wished-for End, tho' they may be proper SIGNETS of Concern: But your *Ethiopian-like Spots* are not to be so slightly washed away. No: You must make use of every Means afforded by Prayer and Fasting, by great Diligence and Watchfulness, in order to arrive at a Conquest over them: Your Heart must, like an ulcerated Wound, be cleansed and purified before it can be healed; and it will be well for you to set about this absolutely necessary Work, before the Time of reconciling yourself to your offended God shall be far from you. Therefore do it To-day, whilst it is called To-day, lest by further Delay you should be more firmly hardened by the Deceitfulness of Sin.

Consider, you were born to die; that you were placed here by your Creator, and endued with a Soul capable of living for ever; and can it be nothing to you, whether you are happy or miserable for ever? Consider again, that you were not only born to die, but that the longest Period of Life's Duration is but like a Grain of Sand upon the Sea-shore, compared to the immensurable Eternity into which you must launch so soon as a Separation of your Soul and Body is made, which may be this Night. And, let this Reflection make you sensible, how much it concerns you to keep from offending him, who can destroy both Body and Soul in Hell, and who may come to execute his Judgments *at a Time when you are not aware*, perhaps at the very

Instant

Inſtant in which you are rioting in ſenſual Pleaſures, and feaſting in thoſe luſcious Joys, which
only leave a Sting behind.

Go to now! you who have thus neglected
God and your Soul, your Huſband, your Children, and your Friends : Go, and conſider your
Ways, that you may thereby be led to alter
your Courſe ; for I would willingly hope you do
not ſee your Follies in ſuch a Light as they are
ſeen by thoſe who feel the Effects of them.

You, perhaps, have never been ſufficiently
verſed in the divine Oracles ; and if not, quick-
ly repair thither, and *draw Water out of thoſe
Wells of Salvation* ; for there you may *buy without Money, and without Price* ; and, for your
better Improvement thereby, procure for yourſelf ſome good and plain Comment thereupon,
or conſult ſome diſcreet Friend, where-ever you
are in doubt. Lay by all your wanton Books
(which are only like Oil thrown upon the
Flames of Luſt, which makes them riſe the
higher) and inſtead of them, reverently turn
over thoſe ſacred Pages, as it is *thoſe, and thoſe
only, which teſtify of God:* There you will be led
by him, who was the *Way* ; be guided by him,
who was *Truth* itſelf ; and be preſerved in your
reformed State, by him who was the *Life and
Light of the World*, through the whole of your
Pilgrimage here, and be made Partaker (when
you have uſed your utmoſt preparative Endeavours) of Bliſs prepared for thoſe that love
God.

You have a great Work to do ; a laborious
Taſk lies before you ; but yet do not be diſ-
couraged

couraged by an Attempt to mend; for (if that is diligently purfued) you will find your Mind exfoliate under the Guidance of the *Sun* of Righteoufnefs, even as the vegetable World does under the Influence of the *Eaftern Rays*.

But (this Work neglected) where can you go in the Day of Tribulation, when Sicknefs and approaching Death comes upon you? You cannot look up with Confidence to God, if, after this Admonition, you perfift to neglect him: You cannot with any Face go to your Friends, whilft you continue in thofe Sins, which alone feparated between you and them: In this Situation, fhould Reflection then take place, yet perhaps God's Patience (*who will not always ftrive with Man*) may appear tired out, and the Pain of your difeafed Body may add Fuel to the Flame of your difturbed Mind, when the direful Expectation of an avenging God, ready to deftroy, haunts your Soul, and fills it with Amazement.

Perhaps you will anfwer to all thefe my Remonftrances, as *Amaziah* did to the Prophet *Amos*, who prophefied *Jeroboam*'s Death in confequence of his Wickednefs, *Go into fome other Land, and there eat Bread, and prophefy there, but prophefy no more at* Bethel.

But do not look upon this as Pedantry or Prieftcraft, for it comes not from one who is ordained to the Office, but only as every one is fo, * who has it at all in his Power *to fave a Soul from Death.* Do not let your Inclination to purfue your Follies make you throw it by as Waftepaper, but read it over at your more ferious and

* Lev. xix. 17.

reflective

reflective Hours (as I am willing to hope you have some) and then I doubt not but, by the Blessing of God upon my weak Endeavours, I may prove an Instrument of your future Comfort, and a Furtherer of your eternal Bliss.

I shall add but two Things more to what I have already wrote, which is, *first*, To point out to you the Progress of Sin, and *secondly*, the Means against it (which perhaps, upon Reflection, you may find to have been the Case with yourself) : Its Progress is thus :

Suggestion draws on Thought, Thought engages Affection, Affection produces Delight, Delight persuades our Consent, Consent advances to act, Acts beget Habits, Habits harden and tempt us to despair of Mercy, Despair defends the Sins it commits ; after which follow, Glorying in Wickedness, Defiance of God, and Contempt of, and scoffing at Religion *, which is, as it were, the Beginning (here) of Damnation itself : To this Pitch you seem almost arrived, and therefore would advise you to retreat immediately, and (*as the Means against Sin*) to call on *Wisdom* †, and to *come unto her as one that ploweth and soweth, and wait for her good Fruits ; thou shalt not toil much in labouring about her, but thou shalt eat of her Fruits right soon. She is very unpleasant to the Ignorant ; he that is without Understanding will not remain with her : But come thou to her with thy whole Heart, and keep her Ways with all thy Power ; for at the last thou shalt find*

* *Parson's* Directory, p. 133.   † Ecclus.
vi. 19, &c.

her

her Reſt, and that ſhall be turned to thy Joy: Or, in the Words of the Poet,

> *To watch and pray, the very firſt*
> *Motions of Sin ſuppreſs,*
> *Conſtantly uſe the Means of* **Grace**,
> *Promoting Holineſs.*

May God, in whoſe Hands are the Hearts of all Men, give you Time and Space for, and alſo the Grace of Repentance: May he influence you by the Means of his powerful Spirit, to ſee your Crimes in a proper Light, and, at the ſame Time, comfort you, when you ſeem to yourſelf overwhelmed in the Ocean of your Iniquity: May he (whenever that happy and neceſſary Minute comes) reach out his ſaving Help to your ſinking, and almoſt deſponding Soul, and graciouſly aſſiſt you by his Right-hand.   I hereby teſtify myſelf

Your Well-wiſher,

29th April, 1753.

THEOPHILUS.

ADVICE

ADVICE

FROM THE

AVIARY:

OR,

The CHANTING MORALIST.

IN

A LETTER from AMATOR to PULCHERIA.

Praise him all ye Fowls of Heaven.

Dear PULCHERIA,

AFTER having congratulated you upon your safe Recovery, at which I very much rejoice, I take the Liberty to send you, for your Amusement, a Pair of Canary Birds, not in the least doubting but they will be well taken Care of.

I hope you will excuse me, if (in order to render them not only a pleasant, but an useful Amusement) I should endeavour to collect together

gether fome of thofe Leffons which they will teach us if we carefully watch them ; not that I think you want many Hints for your Improvement.

1. Their being confined in a Cage, may put us in Mind of the general Confinement of our Natures, which are ever aiming at fomething which now is, and always will be (whilft we are in this World, and till we take our Flight hence) out of our Reach ; and our Confinement is what we cannot (by fluttering about ever fo much) get free from, till we are releafed from the Prifon of the Body.

2. From their Induftry in making their Nefts, we may alfo learn a Leffon of Diligence, to endeavour to provide for ourfelves the proper Neceffaries for our Well-being and Comfort, and the Indulgence of innoeent Pleafures ; it likewife points out how wifely Providence has provided them with Inftinct, inftead of Reafon and Reflection in Man.

3. When you obferve them alternatively to pull and deftroy their own Works, and again and again to arrange them, and can hardly fix them to their Minds ; in this, I think, they plainly exemplify to us that Ficklenefs in our Natures, which is fo apparent, that we fcarcely know how ever to pleafe ourfelves ; and ferves alfo as a Leffon of Contentment at our feveral Allotments.

4. When you hear them fing in the Morning, let them put you in Mind how early we ought to be in our Praife to our Creator ; and how thankfully we (with them) ought to be for every renewed Day, and efpecially after any

par-

particular Deliverance from Danger, or great Illnefs.

They joyfully jump and fing around their Meat when given them ; and thereby hint to us, that all our Provifions fhould be received with Thankfulnefs and Joy, that is, that we fhould fay Grace before Meat.——*N. B.* They do not do fo afterwards ; which fhews, that Satiety is too apt to make us forget the Donor's Hand.

5. If you watch them when they go to Rooft, you will hear them fing a kind of Requiem to themfelves ; which may ferve to put you in Mind, how eafily and refignedly you may go to your Bed, when the Duties of the Day, properly performed, are over.

6. When there are young ones, you will often fee the Hen fed by the Cock (while fhe as it were lays in) ; in which is obfervable, how much Affection and Friendfhip will lead us to do for each other ; efpecially that Affection, Friendfhip, and Complaifance, which ought to fubfift in the married State.

7. It is very inftructive and amufing, to fee how tenderly the Cock and Hen feed the young ones by Turns, and how anxious they feem for their Welfare ; which is a Leffon to Parents in general, to be careful and anxious for the Welfare of their Children ; a Duty this, which I know no-where better performed than by yours.

8. As the young ones begin to be fledged, they alfo are Monitors to us in this Refpect, that we fhould always hope, that he who clothes thefe little Birds, will never leave thofe deftitute

O

for

for whose Amusement they were sent, for whose Sake they were created.

9. Observe the Hen whilst she feeds them, and you will see the utmost Equality, in distributing to them the Food by Turns, without Partiality to one more than to another ; which is a Monition to us, to free ourselves from all Partiality in our Friendships and Affections, where the Merit is equal.

10. It is very observable to see (in case you take one of these little ones away, or that one of them dies) how wretched the old ones are till they have forgot it, which they soon do ; for as their Pleasures are but of a short Duration, so are their Pains too : Let us, with them, also endeavour to set light by reparable Losses, and to value Trifles but as such.

11. When the first Set of young ones fly, you will soon find another Nest of young ones follow ; which it is two to one but they are in Part destroyed by those that were first hatched pecking at them, and endeavouring to starve them : And herein is represented to you a just Picture of the World, full of Jealousy and Ill-nature, continually as it were pecking at, and endeavouring to starve or undermine one another : Now, when you find your Resentment rise against them for these Faults, let it be a Lesson to you of universal Charity and Good-will to others.

In short, the whole Proceedings of them will be a general Lesson (to all) of Gratitude to God, Affection and Love to our Parents ; who have, and do, take infinitely more Pains with us than

is

is neceſſary with theſe little Animals, who have only a *Body* to be provided for, but no *Mind* which wants Cultivation.

You will, by carefully watching them, obſerve a different Language for almoſt every different Employ they ſet each other about ; which may teach you the Neceſſity of learning ſeveral Languages, in order to render yourſelf the more univerſally uſeful.

When you ſee the little Animal in the Shell ſtruggling into Life, and obſerve the Perfection of every Part, it may put you in Mind of your own Creation, and raiſe you up to a due Contemplation of *his* Power who *formed you in the Womb, in whoſe Book all your Members were written, which Day by Day were faſhioned, when as yet there was none of them.*

Their Moulting makes them very ſick, and comes pretty ſudden ; it often kills them ! Hence may be conveyed to us a Monition, to endeavour to be always ready to meet *Sickneſs* or *Death*, that ſo ſhould it come ſuddenly, it may not ſurpriſe us unprepared.

Note well, that you will be very ſubject to have them die, ſo do not ſet your Heart too much upon them ; but, from theſe trifling Diſappointments, endeavour to arm yourſelf with Patience againſt greater.

Was you not the ſenſible and engaging Perſon you are, and had you not a Mind ſufficiently improved to receive this grave Lecture (on a merry Subject) I would have endeavoured to have dreſſed it up in a more juvenile Strain ; but, as I think you qualified, in all Reſpects,

O 2

for any Thing ever so philosophic, I was willing to accommodate my Stile to you in that Way which I thought would best suit your Taste, and, at the same Time, prove a Testimony how ambitious I am to have all the World my Rivals, whilst I subscribe myself

Yours, &c.

AMATOR.

The PROTESTANT's *Universal Prayer.*

O MOST Almighty God, Lord of Heaven and Earth, the supreme Disposer of all Events, the eternal Source of all Being ; thou first uncreated Cause of all Things, and the only beginningless Being ; thou, who in thyself art all glorious, and the only (absolutely) unoriginated Existence ; be pleased to hear the Prayers of thy People ; when they call upon thee,

Hear, O God, from Heaven, thy Dwelling-place, and, when thou hearest, forgive ; receive the Petitions of those who apply to thee in every Exigence, relative, both to their Souls and Bodies, to this Life, or a better.

Give to those who wait at thine Altar, a wise and an understanding Heart, that they (properly interpreting thy holy Word) may give to thy
People

People the *ſincere Milk thereof,* which may bring them up in the Nurture and Admonition of the Lord ; unfold to them (as far as is neceſſary) the hidden *Myſteries* of thy Word, that they may teach it properly to others ; and grant that none of them, whilſt they endeavour to inſtruct others, may ever themſelves prove Caſtaways.

Further : Be thou pleaſed, O Lord, by the Influence of thy Grace, to ſettle the doubtful Mind, and to be the Comfort and Support of the afflicted Soul ; and, by the Force and Power of thy holy, accompanying, aſſiſting, and co-operating Spirit, to convict the Infidel and Obdurate, to direct the Studious, and guide the well-meaning Heart.

Heal, O Lord, the Breaches of thy Church ; thoſe Breaches that have been made through factious Schiſms, or Popiſh Bigotry ; renew to thy Church, and to thy People, the happy Privilege of worſhipping thee in the true Spirit of the Goſpel of thy Son ; grant them that Liberty with which Chriſt has made them free, that they may rejoice therein, when ENTHUSIASM ſhall not put on the *Maſque* of RELIGION, and when *Bigotry* and *Perſecutions* ſhall be no more.

Until which Time, be pleaſed, O Lord, to ſupport thoſe whom thou permitteſt to be ſo ſeverely tried (*that they muſt reſiſt even unto Blood*) that they, following the Examples of the firſt Martyrs in thy Cauſe, may be firm and conſtant, reſolute and bold, and may not, for any Pangs of Death, depart from thee, but may (by thus ſealing thy Truth with their Blood) be entitled,
through

through him in whom they believe, to Bliſs eternal.

Open the Eyes, O Lord, of thoſe blind deluded Creatures, who would endeavour to make us believe, that, whilſt they perſecute others, they do thee Service ; convince them of the Folly of their idolatrous Worſhip, and bring them (and every other who are wandering in the Paths of erroneous Principles in regard to their Religion) back unto thy Flock, that, ſooner or later, in thy good Time, the Heathens, and thoſe that know thee not, may be enlightened, and all the different Perſuaſions in Religion, may be united into one Fold, and be made one Flock under one Shepherd, and may follow the one true Rock, which Rock is Chriſt ; that ſo they may all *concertively* join *here* in religious *Unity*, and *hereafter* in one general and univerſal *Chorus* of Praiſe and Thankſgiving *to God, and to the Lamb, for ever and ever.*

Reſtore, O Lord, thy once favourite People the *Jews*, and make them know that their Redeemer liveth ; and that though he did not come in the *gay Pomp* of a Diadem'd Ruler, yet that he did come (that he has appeared) as they themſelves might have expected he ſhould appear, would they have liſtened to thoſe Types, Prophecies, and Predictions (in thy firſt Revelation to Man) which they themſelves allow and confeſs related to the Messiah ; and if nothing elſe will convince them, let the Reflection on their being now the *diſperſed*, though once the *choſen People* of God ; bring them to an acknowledgment, that that Light hath long ſince appeared,

peared, which was to be the Glory of God's People *Iſrael:* Then may we cordially receive them (thus convicted and converted) into the proper Privileges of the Proteſtant Land.

Give unto the People of this Land (eſpecially the Proteſtants of all Denominations) a kind, benevolent, and charitable Spirit, in regard *to thoſe* who ſhall flee unto us as to the *Horns* of the *Altar,* or a Sanctuary of Refuge; *to thoſe* who, whilſt they are *perſecuted in one City flee unto another*) leaving behind them, for the Sake of their Religion, their Fortunes, their Friends, their Families, and every other Conſolation that could render Life tolerably happy, and who (by ſo doing) clearly ſhew, with St. *Paul,* that *they count all Things but Droſs ſo they may win Chriſt.*

Finally, O Almighty God, be pleaſed to bleſs our moſt gracious Sovereign King *George* (the Defender of our Faith, the Supporter of our Rights, our Liberty and Laws) with the choiceſt of thy Bleſſings here below; continually crown him with Laurels of Victory over his every Foe; grant him a long and peaceful Reign here; and, when thou ſhalt iſſue out thy ALMIGHTY FIAT to call him hence, give him an eaſy Exit out of this Life of Troubles, this Vale of Miſery and Tears; ſeat him at thy own Right-hand for ever, and crown him with thoſe Laurels which will never fade.

Be thou ever preſent at his Counſels, and teach his Senators Wiſdom; and ſo ſhower down thy Bleſſings upon every Branch of his Royal Houſe,

House, that there may never be wanting therein a Man to set upon the Throne of *England*, and in his Stead to stand before thee for ever. *Amen.*

Humanum est errare
Ens entium miserere mei.

F I N I S.

E R R A T A.

Dedication—for *has been* read *may possibly have been.*
Preface—for *modernize* read *methodize.*

CPSIA information can be obtained
at www.ICGtesting.com
Printed in the USA
BVHW082003120819
555665BV00018B/2145/P